DANCING TO THE RHYTHM OF YOUR LIFE

A Happy Becoming Story

Pearl Jordan

Copyright © 2025 by Pearl Jordan

All rights reserved. No part of this publication may be reproduced, distributed or transmitted in any form or by any means without permission of the publisher, except in the case of brief quotations referencing the body of work and in accordance with copyright law.

The content of this book is intended to inform, entertain and provoke thinking. The information given in this book should not be treated as a substitute for professional medical advice; always consult a medical practitioner. Any use of information in this book is at the reader's discretion and risk. Neither the author nor the publisher can be held responsible for any loss, claim or damage arising out of the use, or misuse, of the suggestions made, the failure to take medical advice or for any material on third party websites.

ISBN:

978-1-916529-62-5 (Paperback)
978-1-916529-63-2 (ebook)

Cover design by Lynda Mangoro.

The Unbound Press
www.theunboundpress.com

Hey unbound one!

Welcome to this magical book brought to you by The Unbound Press.

At The Unbound Press, we believe that when women write freely from the fullest expression of who they are, it can't help but activate a feeling of deep connection and transformation in others. When we come together, we become more and we're changing the world, one book at a time!

This book has been carefully crafted by both the author and publisher with the intention of inspiring you to move ever more deeply into who you truly are.

We hope that this book helps you to connect with your Unbound Self and that you feel called to pass it on to others who want to live a more fully expressed life.

With much love,

Nicola Humber

Founder of The Unbound Press

www.theunboundpress.com

Reviews

Wow, wow, totally drawn in, was so raw and touching. I felt so connected and so moved on so many levels. You have created such visually tantalising scenes with words.

Most of us ask ourselves the types of questions you discuss at some stage or age in our lives so that made it interesting from the onset. That said, we are not all brave enough to voice or explore these questions so openly let alone share our experiences or thoughts and reflect on who's tune we might be dancing to, so it pulls you in from the start and invites you to keep reading and discovering.

I loved how you authentically and tentatively guide us through how you arrived at those points of reflection and how you discuss the points that compelled you to take note whether it was an inner voice or outward signs, it draws the reader in and gives food for thought around your own timeline.

I became very invested, I wanted to know more about the little girl, the teenager, the dancer, the woman and the journey. I did find some parts quite emotional because it was so relatable; it was vivid, raw and so honest, it struck a chord.

The flow invites you on a journey. It felt like it was saying I didn't have and don't have the answers, I'm just sharing all these light bulb moments and I'm potentially going to give you insight to how I gave my little inner self a space to shine.

The language you use is very uplifting given that you are (at points) still sharing some fairly deep insightful vulnerable moments in time. I appreciated how you constantly invite the reader to reflect in their own context/world and make the experience their own.

It felt vulnerable in a very engaging way.

- Jo Short

Black — It's great – powerful, poignant, angry and defiant, yet hopeful.

- Mal Peachey, co-author of Don Letts' *There And Black Again*

I found *In The Wings* evocative and active. You capture the energy, anticipation and uncertainty of performance... your writing has such rhythm and momentum.

- Theresa Beattie OBE

Love the poetry and the rhythm of your writing. Adore the dance terminology and the music gifts you give to us the reader, it adds a beautiful sensory layer to the book.

- Vicki Igbokwe-Ozoagu

A jazzy mosaic of prose, poetry, theatre & song, Dancing to the Rhythm of Your Life: A Happy Becoming Story is an exhilarating memoir about Dance - dance as a metaphor for life and self-realisation. Exploring themes such as family, race and ancestry in contemporary Britain, Pearl Jordan skilfully weaves her experience as a jazz dancer & producer into a tapestry that celebrates living life to the full. This is a must read for anyone curious about how to tap into their creativity and excel.

- Yaba Badoe, author of *Man-man and the Tree of Memories, a story of Dance, Magic & Liberty.*

...It's great, a really readable, page turner. Loved the language and structure which took me on a very relatable journey. What an amazing journey you have travelled!

- Marie McCluskey MBE

For you who choose to dance free on the stage of life

Know there is a beam of light guiding your way.

See...

Believe...

Follow...

Introduction

Dancing to the Rhythm of Your Life is designed as a healing journey. It's filled with stories of love, pain, rhythm, laughter and hope.

In this book of transformation and reclamation, Pearl Jordan shares her process of self-rediscovery and how you can awaken to your truth, your unique rhythm and to self-love.

Who are you? Whose dance are you dancing? Are you in tune or out of tune?

As Pearl re-evaluated all areas of her life, the voice of discordant rhythmic beats tapped away and turbulence ensued. Her inner child, no longer suppressed, having been ignored for so long, was now screaming, demanding to be heard, silent no more.

Pearl found that other women were motivated by these themes: women seeking to reclaim their authentic voice, their power, their "Wow!" It inspired conversation, brought clarity of strength and self-acceptance — quirks and all.

Dancing to the Rhythm of Your Life is a Movement; to tune into your inner DJ, to dare to dance to the beat of that rhythm — not somebody else's — on the stage of life.

Dancing to the Rhythm of Your Life

[voiceover]

Enter into a world of stories beneath the story, a personal quest for answers, a journey along the yellow brick road of life. A creative, theatrical path, of self-rediscovery, reflection, challenging the status quo; a meeting of bygone characters and scenes, inner child searching for missing pieces... finding your way 'home'.

Please take your seats.

The Performance is about to begin.

WARNING (NOTICE): Theatrical metaphors and vocabulary are used throughout this storytelling. For those outside the world of theatre and dance, this may prove unsettling. Apologies in advance for any disruptions to your flow. Be assured such interruptions are fleeting with a quickstep back into your groove.

For more information and to ease on down the road, please visit: The Wizard... oops, The Glossary!

Programme

Reviews		5
Introduction		9
Voiceover		11
Prologue		17
Act I: Behind The Scenes		**19**
	Overture	21
	Welcome	22
	...It Is Time...	23
	Niggle Wiggle	25
Scene 1	What's With The Rose Quartz?	26
	M.W. A Return To Love	29
	Vignette for Reflection	34
	Umbilical Cord	35
Scene 2	Once Upon a Dance Floor	37
	Fast Forwards into the Future...	38
	Skip to the Little Girl aged 14 Years Old...	39
	Truth Dances in Happiness	43
	The Power of Truth	44
Scene 3	West Side Story	48
	My Bernstein and Robbins	48
Scene 4	A Question of Love	52
	Back to Regina...	54
	Emotional Absence	55
	What Was Different?	57
Scene 5	Until Death Do Us Part	59
Scene 6	Beaten...	63
	Kwéyòl Etymology	65
Scene 7	Mother-Daughter Healing	66

Scene 8	I Am Blessed	77
	Dance Along	78
	Sassy Oak	79
Act II: The Rehearsal		**81**
	Fame	83
Scene 1	Day One	86
	Pearl's 'Fame'	89
	Rhythm And Rhyme	90
Scene 2	Jazz On Paper	91
Scene 3	To Be Pearl Willie	93
	What's in a Name?	95
Scene 4	Swanee	98
	The Black and White Minstrel Show	99
	The Late 1980s	100
	The Royal Variety Show 1988	105
	Golden Thread	106
Scene 5	Kimmo	108
Scene 6	Pearlicious Cake - A Little Story…	112
	SOS	116
Scene 7	Dancing With the Smell of Fear	118
	Magical Magnificence	122
Scene 8	My Body is My Temple	125
	The Mind-Body Connection	131
	What Was the Magical Remedy?	133
	The Gift of this Time	134
	Your Body is your Temple	136
	Forgiveness	137
Scene 9	Permission to go Solo	139
	Solo…	141
	F.E.A.R	144
Scene 10	Bullies Ballerinas	146
	Vignette	148
Scene 11	Goodbye to Moses	149

Scene 12	Bullies Reborn	153
	Bullies Ballerinas Dance Company Was Born	156
Scene 13	The Hey Days	157
	Reasons, Seasons And Lifetimes (RSL)	163
	Symphony	164
Scene 14	Heartbeat Of Homeopathy	166
Scene 15	Divine Download	170
Scene 16	Angel	174
	Knowing What You Know	176
	Vibrant And Vulnerable	177
Scene 17	Hey Mr Dj	179
Scene 18	A Dance Battle	180
Scene 19	Feeling Great	182
	Moment Of Stillness	185
Scene 20	P.E.A.R.L	186
Scene 21	The Cards Don't Lie	188
	Food For Thought...	191
	Empty Room	192
	What Next...?	194

Act III: In The Wings — 195

Scene 1	Heartbeats	199
Scene 2	Finding Your Groove	201
	Sales	202
	Gift For The Soul	206
Scene 3	Acceptance	207
	A Bridge...	210
Scene 4	Black	212
Scene 5	Sixth Sense	222
	Roll The Camera	223
Scene 6	A Comedy Of Error	230
	The Moral Of The Story?	235
Scene 7	Ti Blackie	239
	Vignette - Feeling Alive!	241
	The Dance Of Happiness	242

Scene 8	Jack Of All Trades	243
	Multi-Passionate	244
	The Truth	245
	Steptoe And Son	246
	Renaissance Woman	248
	Dance Along	251
	Straight Lines	252
Scene 9	A Tale Of Three Augusts	254
	August 2022	254
	August 2023	257
	Trauma	258
	Delete	261
	August 2024	265
	I Will Rise	267
	Where Do I Begin?	268
	Wings	270
	Glow	271
	In The Wings: A Visualisation	272
	Full Circle	276
	Inner Child Peace	277
	Curtain Call	278
	Get Happy	279

Foyer Chit-Chat	280
An Audience With...	287
Applause!!	294
Glossary	299
Resources	303
Music Catalogue	305
Book References	311
About The Author	312

Dancing to the Rhythm of Your Life

Prologue

She who took the shackles off her feet so she could dance
Felt the niggle wiggle
Offering her a new chance
A journey of untold ails prevailed
With which to set sail
The seas at times fraught
Provided much that she sought
A Rhapsody of Delights
To dance however she likes
No rules rule
Now she stands in the wings
Free as a bird
That's how her 'fat lady' sings
It ain't over 'til her light of day
Shines forever brightly
Bouquet…
Broadway…
Wot to say…

Act I

BEHIND THE SCENES

[overture]

Take the shackles off my feet so I can dance

I just want to praise you

I just want to praise you

You broke the chains

Now I can lift my hands

And I'm gonna praise you

I'm gonna praise you...

Shackles (Praise You)

Artist: Mary. Mary

Welcome to Dancing to the Rhythm of Your Life, your 'R.O.Y.L' I like to say. A journey of unexpected 'joy and pain like sunshine and rain' steps on the turbulent road to self-rediscovery.

I could say I consciously instigated this path, but I did not. I would have run a mile and *boogie-backed* into a corner had I known then what I know now.

I must have had a deep calling for change, a ting a ling a ling, bell ringing parts of me recognising it was time to face stuff, hidden suppressed stuff, stuff that I didn't even know was there.

But there comes a time, doesn't there, when you are ticking along nicely and then wham! You get the niggles. You don't know what those niggles are, but they niggle enough to stop you in your tracks, right? Get you thinking, feeling, checking in, and eventually, when the niggle becomes loud but you deny its existence, its exploration, and expression, you are compelled to take stock. No more running away.

It is time to start the Ali shuffle towards your inner opponent.

For it is time...

There is a part of you, as there is a part of me that knows, knows when it is the next season of your life, a niggle nudge time.

Call it your inner knowing; something that compels you to listen, pause, reassess, renew.

To glide into the next phase of 'who am I?'

Gradually I've come to recognise those niggles. In my case they reach out and touch every few years before a new decade 30s! 40s! 50s! 60s! Preparing for the death of one era and the life of another.

The call of rebirth is at hand...

...It is Time...

Time to get back on track

to listen to those ringing bells

to tap into your inner voice,

those whispers

restoring balance,

into the joy of your life.

It

          is

                    Time

Time to get bright and breezy

to make your life so much more easy

yeast

rising

expanding

purpose

into the bread of your life... yum!

It

          is

                    Time

Time for you to simply be

reclaim renewed energy

have a greater sense of yourself

to be at peace with yourself

kind to the self

best friends with yourself

yes, BEST FRIENDS with yourself.

It

                                      is

                                                                        Time

To nurture

commit

to care to swing dance with it

your inner ROYL creating music

first a nudge

then the niggles,

how can you enable your wiggle?

It

                                      is

                                                                        Time!

NIGGLE WIGGLE

What

does

it

take

for

you

(enter name)

to

listen

to

your

niggle

and

dance

to

the

rhythm

of

your

life?

What's with the Rose Quartz?

Have you ever found yourself ticking along nicely then out of the blue a turning point presents itself?

The Wish

If only I'd realised.

The Wish is a board game presented on a luxurious, deep violet fabric.

At the start you make a wish, and then you work your way round and collect cards that prompt you, think Monopoly, but instead of a property portfolio at the end, you are presented with a final 'your wish is my command' message guiding you towards your desire.

The lovely Denise. I met her at a networking event. Her 'Genie and the lamp' your wishes come true one minute pitch, had me hooked. A board game that takes you on a transformational journey…? Yes, please. I'm having some of that! Plus, her voice had the familiar Cypriot style tones of my dear friend Martha, so that was it. Another reason to be sold.

Signed up, I met with a group of women at a Boutique Hotel in Central London. The set up was as luxurious as the deep violet fabric. We sat around tables in small groups of four or so and skipped along the board, moving forwards, backwards, down a snake, up a ladder, you get my drift… actions typical of board games that take you on an emotional ride of 'yes!!' and 'Aaarh!'

At the end of the game, I was presented with a final card: Rose Quartz.

I knew of the Rose Quartz. It's a pinkish stone, and many moons ago a Feng Shui practitioner suggested I buy small pieces to place around the electrical sockets of my home, to reduce the negative impact of EMF (electromagnetic frequency). That was all I knew.

The Wish facilitator however smiled and said, "Ah, the stone of Love."

'Hmm... that's nice' thought I, and nothing more to it.

A year later, I treated a friend to experience The Wish. Together we played and at the end of the game I received a card, and yes, Rose Quartz.

"What's with the Rose Quartz?" I asked the facilitator.

"I don't know, you're the one who continues to choose that card. Has anything love-based shown up for you since you last played?"

I hadn't really thought about it. But now, clearly something was going on...

"You may wish to look into this more deeply."

Hmmm...

I started to think about how fortunate I was to be in a loving, long term relationship, how I had the love of family and friends... Well then, all was good, and so I left it at that.

Bang!

A few months later I'm with friends and as we walk past a bookshelf in the street, a book falls at my feet. I pick it up and it's titled *A Return to Love*. You couldn't make it up. The universe was at play!

My friend said: "Oh that's an amazingly powerful book by Marianne Williamson — the spiritual teacher."

Oh, said I, attempting to be nonchalant, but of course it hit home. There it was, LOVE again!

> *"What is this thing called love, that*
> *funny thing called love?"*
>
> *- Cole Porter*

That song, in Ella Fitzgerald Jazz Singer style, was whirling in my head, swirling hypnotically. There was no more ignoring... but... shrug it off I did.

"Why Pearl?! Why?!" I hear you, but consider this:

Have you ever had something look you hard between the eyes and pretend you can't see?

Have you ever received messages and ignored, procrastinated, pretended to be unaware?

If you have, you know what I am talking about.

Could it be that deep down, you knew change was calling?

That you would have to face your fears, because that's what it's about, isn't it? Always a fear lurking in the background, even if it's an unconscious fear, it is always there. And you are not convinced that you have the strength to deal with what's around the corner, so you avoid, and by the way, often none of this is conscious decisioning. It's all playing behind the scenes.

Ring a bell...?

On reflection, that was going on with me.

Not consciously, but deep within my inner self my soul knew it was time. Time to get back on track, to listen to those ringing bells. AND that I was ready.

Even if I didn't know it, 'we' were ready to face suppressed trauma in my life, one that would turn my world upside down, with no immediate end in sight.

"OK.

"You're not listening", sighs the universe and then...

M.W. A Return to Love

I am waiting to attend a salsa class with my best friend Jeanefer. We have arrived early and are killing time with a snack and drink in a bar restaurant. I am aglow with excitement! Salsa is now our 'thing', visiting various clubs, dancing the night away. The class is due to take place above the restaurant. Neither of us have been there before, and we have yet to visit again since that magical, surreal night.

She is walking towards me, making her way through the restaurant...

Marianne Williamson.

Time slows down, and in my head, I am like "Oh my, oh my, sort of like, can't catch my breath, my brain is zinging, oh my, oh my!!!!"

At this point I know who she is, not only because the book fell at my feet, but I'd since watched her in full *Super Soul Sunday* glory, with none other than, Oprah.

YES, the universe thrusts Marianne Williamson onto my path!!!

As she walks past, our eyes meet and... I accost her.

I still don't understand how I convinced her to sit with me, but I remember stroking her arm and apologising for doing so.

Magic.

The universe at play.

We speak of different things; she's in town, hanging out, had no idea about a salsa class. She asks about me, we talk about creativity and my unique approach to dance, and Marianne says in that lyrical American accent way: "Sounds like you're doing *transformational dance*".

My jaw drops. She blows my mind!

Transformational Dance?... Did she say *Transformational Dance*?!

In an instant, Marianne Williamson described my process with movement and dance in a way I had never thought of before. And it was years before I truly embraced what that meant. But more on that later.

I learned that Marianne was at a loose end and was due to leave for America in a week, so I asked her "No event planned?" Apparently not.

Then, I heard the words, "I'll do it. I'll produce an event for you."

Marianne looked at the individual incredulously, "OK-ayyy?"

"Yes, I can do that. I can produce an event for you," says she.

And before you know it, I, Pearl Jordan, now producer, God help me, exchanges contact details with the great M.W.

...And they are off!

[Deep breath]

She looked at me as if I was cRaZy, then she gave me her private number — her private number! Jean and I laughed throughout salsa class that evening: I was going away Friday, Saturday, Sunday and Marianne was going away the following Friday so when I came back on the Monday I had three days: Monday, Tuesday, Wednesday to find a venue, do the whole thing. So I called all the friends that I could think of and said "HEEEEEELLLLP! Gotta get it out on social media I don't know how to do social media, gotta sell tickets online HoW?!" Meanwhile, I started communicating with Marianne and her PA in America all these procedures oh my goodness it was hysterical! Was I CRAZY...?! I found a venue in Covent Garden, fandabbydozy! I negotiated the costs, got my team, put it out there and in fact NO, *[tearing hair out]* I tried stalling to get all systems and details in place before I put it out there but instead the great M.W. put it out there and bOom in a split second of star spangled fireworks the word was out, and London was ablaze with fans demanding tickets NOW! *[Oxygen please!!]* The venue was inundated and irritated by the endless calls, I'm negotiating with America, Marianne and her super excited mob in the UK, plus the venue... oh Lawd! Anyway, it all came together, was a sell-out event, queues around the block, who is that for... oh it's our gig! Crowds standing outside in the hope of a late entry. "What next? Who next?" I was asked. And I was like, "NO. This is a one-off, NO. Thank you thank you all the same."

We made it over the finishing line!

[Exhale]

Magic.

The universe at play.

First the Rose Quartz, stone of love, and now the queen of love. What more did I need?

It was time to buy the book *A Return to Love* and I...

Cried... and cried.

Tears free flowing, boo-booing, overflowing, at every whim.

Every word pinging at my heart. Every chapter creating a momentous awakening, a wealth of emotion rising, falling, reconfiguring all preconceptions of love. And self- love at that!

Since when did I not love myself? Of **course** I love myself.

And so why the tears? I was on a spiritual journey. For several years I had been practising Raja Yoga Meditation, a meditation without rituals or mantras and accessible to people of all backgrounds. Having explored various techniques previously, I considered it a blessing to have found this very practical form, a meditation practise with 'open eyes', meaning you can meditate anywhere at any time.

I remember in the early days when I attended an event at the meditation centre and heard the beautiful voice of an angel singing a song called *A Hundred Thousand Angels*. That voice belongs to my now very dear friend, singer songwriter, Lucinda Drayton.

Listening to Lucinda sing with her healing dulcet tones, I was surprised to find tears rolling down my cheeks. Thank goodness I was sat in a corner with subdued lighting.

And now, here I was again. In that very same space with the book, A Return to Love', weeping, weeping. Grit and inner child stuff appeared to be bubbling in a re- evaluation of all things, pushing and pulling a tumbleweed of emotions.

This I believed to be an invitation to enter into the studio of my life, to explore steps of the past, with steps of the present; to reassess what my rhythm truly was and to, fingers crossed, get back on beat.

What if I were to dance from the premise of lacking in love?

What might that bring?

At worst, it was true, at best, confirm me flourishingly, love-full!

I would avoid no more.

I came to understand there were Inner Child parts fretting to be heard, held, nurtured, nourished and loved for who they are rather than the versions they had learnt to become; a cadence influenced by so many beats.

She the toddler. She the infant child, the teenager, twenty-years-old me, 30, 40, perimenopausal (watch out) me, 50, 60 years old wisdom me; all parts presenting their needs in imperfectly perfect, healing ad hoc order.

Wow.

It's funny how, in my innocence I thought, "I'm in a loving relationship, I have the love of my family my friends, why the Rose Quartz?"

Isn't it interesting how I looked outside of me first? That my conditioning and potentially yours too, is to look in another direction, to veer towards the external, as the first port of call: "I love my partner, I love my family, friends…"

It would have never occurred to me without the universe nudges, that it was time for a 'selfie'.

Inside out. Not outside in.

The lens focused back on me.

And so, it proved…

The journey that followed involved years of swimming in muddy waters, coming up for air and presenting as an illumined Lotus flower every now and then.

Years of retreating into my shell, in that pearl oyster irritation and agitation way, layer upon layer of neutralising challenges and struggles; until such time that… Ta-da! Presenting, "Pearl, renowned for bringing joy, energy and enthusiasm to any stage!"

I believe the dance of destiny was truly at play; the meditation, the insistence of the rose quartz, and the whole M.W. story, all 'Pearl drops' destined to fall into place.

This was the seed of my Transformational Dance.

And here I am today planting, nurturing, propagating with you.

VIGNETTE FOR REFLECTION

Let					Way

   Love				The

     Lead			Lead

       The		Love

         Way Let

What if your intellect were to fly on the wings of love?

If you were to fly on the wings of love,
how would that show up for you...?

UMBILICAL CORD

I was born with the umbilical cord around my neck.

I knew I had made a mistake.

No, please, stop, I've changed my mind.

I want to go back in time.

Mistake, mistake.

But too late,

Strangled before I could be welcomed to my Earth Day,

A sign of things to come…

In utero,

Pearl

Here I stand in a centred, knowing open-hearted way for the benefit and the love of you. Because in the words of James Brown, "I feel good... I knew that I would... so good, so good, I've got you." And to be able to share this with you means the world to me.

Today I dance my dance my way,
but it wasn't always the case...

Once Upon a Dance Floor

Once upon a dance floor there was a little girl dancing, surrounded by a forest of legs. She must have been small because she remembers the kneecaps so high. The forest of legs was jigging to the rhythms of the Soca beat, the heart of calypso, and everyone was dancing to their merry tune. The little girl was dancing free, lost in the joy of the pounding beat, when something changed. Suddenly, there was an opening...

The little girl realised that she was centre stage. All eyes upon her, staring in amazement. There was applause as she looked up, her mind a buzz with confusion.

"Why are they staring at me? What have I done?"

And then she realised, they were celebrating her.

The 'forest of legs' were celebrating her dancing.

But the little girl, instead of embracing the moment and doing a child star Shirley Temple — lapping up the limelight, she felt exposed, awkward. She didn't like nor recognise this feeling. It made her very uncomfortable.

In that moment the little girl moved from a place of innate power, a place of shining her light, to a place of confused darkness, fear and hiding.

She didn't like it.

Didn't know what to do with the appreciation. You could say a glimpse of 'love'.

She couldn't relate to it and scurried away into the forest, hiding the ball of light deep within.

Her 'permission to be powerful' having been stripped away.

What was it that made her keep running away?

What had she learnt so early on in life?

Fast forwards into the future…

She went to tap lessons — "you can do it" — but she ran away.

She was on the stage at the London Palladium, singled out for her talent, and she ran away.

She was on the verge of trailblazing recognition, with a view to creating the first ever London jazz dance festival, and she, all together now… "ran away!"

You can only do that for so long don't you think before you sing, in the words of Donna Summers, "enough is enough. I can't go on, I can't go on, no, no, no".

Enough already.

How many times must I run away in my life?

How many times *have you* run away…?

Indeed, what is your version of 'running away…?'

Me? I had to take stock.

To boogie on back and check in on what was going on.

I was in this repetitive cycle, that crept up sneakily every time. It was not serving me, and it was time to step back.

Skip to the little girl aged 14 years old...

It's careers day at school and nothing appeals. She doesn't want to be a nurse, a teacher or anything the career adviser suggests. She is lost and disheartened. It's summer break; she finds a book in the library — something strange called *Hatha Yoga*. Throughout the summer she practises the yoga postures with great enthusiasm and by the end of the school holidays she can sit in the Lotus position. She is proud of herself.

Back at school, happy days. As if by magic, a new teacher arrives; a dance teacher called Jennifer Frankel (now Silverton). She is passionate, full of energy and enthusiasm. She loves to dance, and she encourages, nurtures and brings such joy to the daily grind of school. Be it fate, be it coincidence, the coming together of *Hatha Yoga* and Ms Frankel reawakens that little dancing child and her power.

The confused 14-year-old is confused no more. She has gone back to her roots, reconnected to her joy of dance and has given herself permission to be powerful again.

Before you know it, in fact, by the age of 17, she's assisting Jenny — yes, now on first name terms (rebel Jenny) — and running dance clubs; teaching groups of 90 plus young people, passing on the power of dance.

She hits the national and international press after a chance meeting with HRH Prince Charles, now King Charles III. She has just performed as part of a youth Commonwealth programme at the then County Hall, and there is a steel band playing calypso, and she has the nerve to call him over, "Oi, Prince Charles, do you want to learn a disco dance?" And disco dance he does. They 'click-click' together. How could he refuse her charm?

She attends WAC (Weekend Arts College), a performing arts college way ahead of its time. With a trailblazing approach to empowering young people through the arts, founder Celia Greenwood becomes a mentor in all areas of her life. She is ignited and inspired even more.

A Bachelor of Arts Honours Degree follows. Thank you tutor Wendy Cook, for having the insight to see beyond the 'crazy' young black girl doing her best to dance in a contemporary style to the soca beats of 'Let me Love You'. It must have been a first! Lol!

DANCE feeds her soul. It fires her up with a daring confidence and spark.

There is only one path for her to take, and this is to step to her beat and move into the world of professional dance.

Until such time...

"That's it. I've had enough! I will never be good enough. Nothing about me matters. I'm too stiff, my butt is too big, my thighs too bulky, just not turned out enough, can't even do the splits, glare of utter disdain. It's time to give up!"

Tenacity and resilience out of the window!!

Professional training in a new environment was taking its toll on her mental health. At her audition she was told to get rid of 'them', them being her 'bulky thighs and black butt'. Not the actual words but the pointing finger was clear. It was way back in the 1980s, elite privilege was in the air, her physical body was not welcome here. "Promise to get rid of them, and you can join us."

"Yes, I promise," she urged gratefully. And get rid of them she certainly did.

No more starchy yam, dasheen, sweet potato Caribbean foods.

Endless stretching of muscles and squeezing her buttocks until they flattened into insignificance.

"Pearl, what's happened to your backside? Where's it gone?!" exclaimed aunt Titi Bethalina in dismay.

This should have been a warning sign. A sign of things to come.

Within a short time, she was completely stripped of her confidence, her spark and love of dance. Her unique qualities once her driving force, appeared to count for very little, no matter how many times she hit 5,6,7,8. Get ready, Go!

And unbeknown to her, building in her mind, or shall I say her heart, that old memory and a desire to run away, for her shine was not welcome here.

But then, just as with Hatha Yoga and the arrival of Jenny at school, an earth Angel appeared... Deidre Lovell.

We called her Dee. A bolshie, female American Horton jazz dance teacher, choreographer. Dee was unapologetic in every way, vocally, physically, with a 'here I am, take me or leave me' attitude I had never witnessed before. She was black! Sassy! With a pronounced butt (yes!!!!), arms and legs that stretched forever. Dee was syncopation personified, with African American jazz roots pumping through her core, her every step and beat! She was alive with soul, and I could feel my black-self screaming, YES! YES! At last! More of you please! In YOU I see ME, but the *powers that be have no interest in that version of me.*

"That's it. I've had enough! I will never be good enough. Nothing about me matters. I'm too stiff, my butt is too big, my thighs too bulky, blaa di blaa di blaa!"

"What's with you Pearl?" Dee was astute. She could read the battle within me.

"I feel broken, as if nothing I do is right. Every day feels like another reason to give up. My body struggles with what they are demanding of me. All the girls are loose, you might as well say double jointed, and I am so tight physically. I love ballet but I will never be a ballet dancer. I appreciate the need for ballet to help broaden my understanding of dance, but I will never be a ballet dancer and have no wish to be," I cried.

"And so, what do you know about you? What type of dancer are you, the style that lights up your life?" As if she didn't know. "Stop allowing yourself to be moulded into something you are not. Why are you allowing them to break you? Remember who you are, your strengths, your passion, and be that way!"

Actually, Dee said very little of the polite above. I thought it easier on your ears to give you this nice clean version. What she did do was ask the first question and then shift into a no nonsense, expletive version that whipped me back to my truth!

TURNING POINT, like a pirouette in action. A quick 360 degree turn back to my truth.

I look back at that moment and see what Dee did for me. She gifted me the best wakeup call ever.

Be true to who you are. Only you really know the answer to that. What touches your heart...?

Rhythm! Staccato! ***Jazz hands!!!!***

Well, done.

TRUTH DANCES IN HAPPINESS

May you be a great powerful soul with the power of truth who constantly dances in Happiness.

It is said where there is truth the soul dances.

Those who are truthful, that is those who have the power of truth will constantly dance, they will never wilt, become confused, be afraid or feel weak.

They will constantly be dancing in happiness.

They will be powerful.

They will have the power to face everything

Truth never fluctuates. It is unshakable.

The boat of truth may rock but it will never sink.

So you souls who imbibe the power of truth, are great souls.

- Raja Yoga Meditation

The Power of Truth

What do you think happened to my ballet...

    a) Things continued to go from bad to worse?
    b) I excelled?

To my great surprise, I **excelled**! I even received a Gold Star!!!!!

Fancy that.

"Stop the class," announced the ballet teacher who had previously tortured me innumerable times. "Pearl, return to the corner and dance the diagonal once again."

I looked to him expecting the usual scowl, but on this occasion... he smiled.

"You receive the gold star!"

Say what...?!!

*My eyes **popping** out of my head*

taking in this surreal moment of accolade.

I swirl round, strut to the corner

and take my centre stage!

I remember that day, as if yesterday, dancing across the diagonal, a regular feature of a dance class.

The 'diagonal' can be such a scary place, but it's a great space for building confidence, and overcoming insecurities.

You all line up as an ensemble in the designated corner of the studio. You are amongst others, you are all learning the same thing, so there is a comfort in that, knowing that you are all in the same boat together.

And you are **exposed**.

The exposure is that you are about to travel across the floor solo or perhaps with one other person, with all eyes on you. That's the scary bit that tells you so much about you.

- Will you boldly take the first step, go for it and lead?
- Will you place yourself in the safety of the middle?
- Will you hide at the back?

And then once you've managed to get your brain cells in order and have made your way across the floor, now it is time to reverse the whole thing, do it on the opposite side!

There are many parallels between the diagonal and life.

- Are you comfortable leading the way?
- How are you with exposure and having to think fast on your feet?
- Do you wait for others to raise a hand in response to a question and then follow suit?

These are common themes, a universal experience. What are your examples?

Prior to my gold star day, the diagonal represented stress and deep ballet insecurities. But once I had reclaimed my sense of self, my truth, the diagonal became my friend. With self-empowerment and self-belief reinforced, there was no stopping me.

This is a general guide for us all isn't it?

Reclaim your sense of self, your confidence and truth, then bingo, full steam ahead.

Thank you, Dee!!

Interesting isn't it? It was never about ballet per say, it was my stress response, and a shut down due to outside pressures. The dance limits were all in the mind, but once I reclaimed **me** and let go of the outside looking in, **freedom** ensued in my mind, body, and spirit, crushed for so long now once again dancing free!

> *"What are **you** willing to **give up** in order to have the life you **keep on pretending** you would like?"*
>
> - Unbound Writer's Podcast Episode 176: Book-writing lessons from Elizabeth Gilbert

...Give up... pretending...?

Deep...

I had let go of my true vision and had adopted a charade. Giving up on the pretence was the best thing ever.

Have you been in this 'ballet' space, or are you now?

What can you do to turn things around?

A ballet dancer dances 'en pointe'. What makes you or will help you to dance your life 'on point' today?

The Sole aim of movement should be joy and flowing energy.

Movement makes energy start to flow.

Flowing energy loosens blockages in the body, head and heart.

Loosened blockages release joy and strength.

Released joy helps us to stay healthy or get healthy throughout the body,

mind and soul.

Stiffening is the basis of death,

movement the basis of life.

Moon Time

- Johanna Paungger and Thomas Poppe

West Side Story

Have you heard of *West Side Story*? The musical adaptation of *Romeo and Juliet*, directed and choreographed by Jerome Robbins. **SO** on point!

I was introduced to *West Side Story* as a child, and when I first heard those rhythmic opening musical notes, it was like all parts of me jumped alive, an awakening, like truth pumping through my veins; like that moment of dancing surrounded by the forest of legs to the rhythmic beat of soca music.

My Bernstein and Robbins

Pow, Zap!

A sigh, a tear or two.

That pleasant hangover feeling, swaying a swoon and no booze.

I have conquered Everest, I am on a high, so high.

They say, "Get well soon" They just don't understand why

You are my pick me up,

You give me hope,

I am nourished by your food.

Bursts of excitement beyond belief,

I've something special,

We've all got this 'special'

That something special is magic to me.

It is hilarious. This I found hidden in a box up in the loft. My ode to *West Side Story*.

I remember writing this poem as a performing arts student in the early 1980s. Whenever I felt low or despondent I would go to the remedy of West Side Story, watch the dance scenes and feel completely rejuvenated afterwards.

One day I thought to write about it and here it is, showing up at this time; my rhythmic healing, catalyst, full of contrasting, genius beats.

Rhythm was certain to be a powerful expression of me. Is it any wonder I became a jazz dancer? Lol!

Goldie Hawn, during a televised Oprah Masterclass, speaking about dancing as a child said: *"When they played the music, I forgot everything, and I danced, and I had the best time... And I knew that I could fly to the beat, to the tone of what I heard of my own drum, and I wanted to feel the expression of the music freely and unencumbered..."*

Oh, how I could relate to that very thing! Flying to the beat of your own drum, lost in the rhythmic bliss of dance, moving unencumbered, free, no rules, no permission required, pure surrender, truth leading the way.

The dance of life in full swing.

Playtime, free style...

Clap a rhythm that represents you today. Go on, no time to think. Trust your gut. Put down your book and clap a rhythm that represents your truth.

Is it fast, slow, irregular, off-beat, syncopated, hesitant?

What does it tell you, ask of you today?

What about a colour?

What does it signify?

What's the message?

Now grab your 'feel good', your happiness, your favourite dance music or even James Brown's *I Feel Good* and shimmy your feet intoxicatingly spellbound.

No running away.

Only towards.

Give yourself permission to stand in your **centred**, **knowing**, **open-hearted** way, for the benefit and the love of you...

...and dare to dance
your dance
your way.

Dearest (enter name),

You are cordially invited to follow your passion

to recognise your talents

to be the star of your own story

to sing your heart out dance your socks off

and to voice your voice your way.

Are you in?

RSVP You bet!

A Question of Love

I was born and raised in West London in the old borough of Paddington, W9, referred to as mini-Saint Lucia (Loo-Shaa).

Every next door belonged to an aunt, uncle, or cousin, or a person from the village 'back home'.

My young self believes there to have been no locks on the doors, but I think it was the tight sense of community that prevailed. Everyone knew everybody, and everyone, as we St. Lucians like to say, "was in everybody else's business!"

You'd collect carrots from Auntie Jane, bring yams to Titi Edmay, Tata or Auntie Mary, there was lots of sharing, to-ing and fro-ing and many, many, parties. We danced to the music of calypso, soca, reggae, even the country and western music of Jim Reeves was in the mix. The St. Lucians love a bit of country and western! And there was always a reason to eat, drink, and dance.

My mother was an 'Edmund'. There were many of them. It was great to be an Edmund. You went to primary school with a clear instruction: "someone hits one, you all hit back!" And so we did. We didn't go looking for trouble, but if it came, all the Edmunds would pounce. The Edmunds looked after their own and looked out for those in their inner circle. We were a clan to be reckoned with and I loved it!

It's important to say I was lucky to have both parents in my life; Moses and Regina Willie. Both incredibly strong, proud and able individuals juggling jobs to keep us, me and my four siblings (Mary, Celia, Keith and Roger) fed, clothed and watered.

My parents were of the Windrush Generation, people of the Caribbean invited to help rebuild post-war Britain.

Together with hundreds and thousands, they left their slow-paced, sunshine, and blue sea Island of St. Lucia. They travelled to the 'Motherland', UK, the Great British Empire, with the promise of a better life in London, the city with roads paved with gold.

If there was gold, it was hidden. The immigrants received a welcome that couldn't be further from the truth.

They experienced racism, struggle, abuse, but they, my parents, held focus. 'Moses and Regina', hear those names: Prophet and Queen — 'The regal feminine'. There was no "go back to your country" for them. They had vision, a clear intent. They were to be the creators of their fortune, and nothing was to prevent them from reaching their 'gold'.

My father was a constant presence, strong, stubborn, with a capital S!!! He was bright, intelligent, easy going, old skool strict, opinionated, with twinkling eyes. I loved that over the years people would say, "you can tell you are Moses' daughter; you have his smiley eyes".

Moses arrived as a tailor by profession but, as with many immigrants, he soon had to let go of that skill and became a painter and decorator, an excellent one at that. He was incredibly creative, and we lived in 'The Black and White House'. Everyone knew 'The Black and White House' with white brick work and black pointing, tastefully designed with great pride.

My mother Regina was bright and educated, she would read letters for the illiterate, was finance savvy and the community banker, who held 'The Partner'.

People of the Caribbean had to become resourceful because no bank would provide them with a loan, so they created their own system. 'The Partner' was known as 'Bayja' to us, but my understanding is that it can hold a different title, depending on the island.

It's ingenious.

The Partner has a number of 'hands', i.e. people who deposited weekly an agreed sum, say £10. Ten Hands would produce £100 per week and on an agreed rota, one individual would receive the full £100 'hand'.

It was a system that allowed them to save and pay for their bills, rent, holidays etc. And it's important to understand that in the 1950s /60s some were earning £5 a week so they had to find a way to survive financially, and the 'Partner' was the saving grace. Several partners would be on a role at once, you really had to stay on top of those figures.

I hear from my sister Celia that today the 'Partner' system still exists, and she holds several 'hands'. I am astonished and pleased at the same time. It's wonderful that the Caribbean community are still rooted in this.

A bit of trivia but valuable... she also mentioned the Metropolitan Police are now aware of this banking system. Prior to this, on searching a property and finding lots of cash, they often assumed money laundering and had to be convinced otherwise.

Thank goodness for education and a change in perspectives today.

Back to Regina...

She was super old skool strict, opinionated, St. Lucian loud and proud. She ruled the roost, was the go-to person for advice, or the saviour to many cousins who had been thrown out of the house by their parents. It didn't take much to have you and a bin liner full of your clothes being shown to the door!

She was generous, openhearted, very religious (Catholic) and creative. She crocheted the most amazing items, including a lovely baby blue skirt and pink top I clearly remember wearing as a child; the outfit, one each for me, my sister Celia and cousin Luna. My mother and her sister, Tata, Luna's mother, had a habit of dressing us like triplets. This still amuses us today!

And as for cake. Lucky for us, Mummy was the local baker. Our home was forever filled with the aroma of baked wedding, christening, holy communion cakes. The designs were elegant and as for the tastings... Yum! How I still LOVE CAKE!! It brings such happy memories.

***

Regina and Moses were highly respected and strong leaders. They were no-nonsense people, with a sense of self that I believe equipped them to survive and thrive within both the hostile and opportune environment of the UK.

They were also, it could be said, highly entrepreneurial.

My mother juggled a morning and evening cleaning job plus she was the community number one 'celebrity' child-minder during the day. Our home was constantly full of children, many of whom became honorary siblings. My father held employed and self-employed decorating jobs. They worked hard. They had five children to provide for, a mortgage to re-pay and the responsibility of consistently sending funds 'back home' to support their families and to buy land for that future vision of returning home, which I am proud to say they actually achieved in August 1985.

But the getting there must have been tough. I'm exhausted thinking about it!!

And there was a price to pay.

Emotional Absence

It's not that my parents lacked emotion, they were very alive, but what was missing in our household were hugs and lovey-dovey ways of being.

We were loved, for certain we were. It showed up in keeping a roof over our heads, instilling values and good manners, keeping us clean, clothed, watered and fed. We were fed like kings and queens, my mother renowned for the feasts she provided. Even now as a vegetarian, the thought of her seasoned roast chicken… mmmm, licking my lips!

Ours was a household of tough love, it could be said. There was no room for that softly, softly, love you, appreciation stuff.

Their approach to nourishment and nurture came from the knocks of life — get up and get on with it.

If they arrived with the Caribbean warm, full of hope, sunshine within their hearts, the British 'cold' soon froze that.

Love has many faces.

Different cultures express in their unique way.

No one heart fits all.

The mistake is in believing it to be so.

Moses was easy in his flow of life. He took our family, including cousins, to many a seaside trip, regular swimming picnic Sundays, and even to Brussels and Calais, which was huge. People in our community just didn't do that. Daddy had adventure. That was his lovey-dovey!

Regina, Mummy, on the other hand, in my opinion — not wishing to offend my siblings who may have seen things differently — appeared angry and irritated.

I will raise my hand and say in her defence, that it may not have been anger, but her no-nonsense, direct Lucian way that presented as such.

She may have also been exhausted, juggling three jobs a day, managing husband, house and home.

Wouldn't you be?

It is sad to say however that this energy impacted our mother-daughter relationship. We didn't really have one. We could be in each other's company, speak, even laugh, especially in her later years when she had returned to St. Lucia, but we never ran deep.

It got to the point where to make a phone call, I'd have to summon the courage to dial her number, praying that we'd have something substantial to talk about. And you know what? Nine times out of ten, we did.

This said more about me and what was going on in my head and heart, then it did about her.

I was the one with mind games playing havoc. The one that entertained monkey chitter chatter.

I was the one struggling with long overdue unresolved stories, the one still playing the child, not brave enough to be the adult and have the conversation.

I was the one not willing to speak her truth and pain.

And I was angry and sad.

There was one moment, a full, whole week in St. Lucia, that Mummy and I spent alone with no other siblings to fill 'the void', just the two of us. And it was amazing. We were so at ease with each other. I loved every minute of it!

What was different?

Perhaps something in me, perhaps being more accepting of who she was, but I also had to thank Oprah and Dr Phil!!

Dr Phil appeared on Oprah as a relationship and life coach-type expert. My mum was in love with Dr Phil. He opened her eyes to a new world and way of thinking and problem solving. Her mantra became (and please imagine a strong West Indian accent):

"Well, Dr Phil sez... Dr Phil would sey... Did you hear what Dr Phil sed...?"

I loved having Dr Phil in my mum's life! She became more open, her world completely transformed by Dr Phil and Oprah insights.

She was light and happy with life, and it was clear she loved having me there with her.

That was a special time I will forever cherish.

Until Death Do Us Part

In January 1993 my father suddenly passed away. I was shocked and devastated.

He went from being the ever strong, muscular man, whose torso I once walked along as a child to ease his muscles, to a stroke-induced, wiped out individual.

He was aged 60 with so much potential ahead, working his banana plantation, and as entrepreneurial as ever. He and my mother had built an impressive property in the lush hills of the capital, Castries; a building with a top floor large enough to house their five children and families, plus a ground floor establishment.

'Morne Fortune Guest House and Restaurant' it was proudly named. A buzzing environment rich with the flavours of the Caribbean; food, drink, loud gospel, country and western, rap, afro-beat, reggae, soca and pop music all in the mix, blaring from passing cars and 'transports', the local buses.

As you sat on the balcony, you'd receive the daily bird song greetings of "good morning, good afternoon, good evening" from passers-by young and old, Lucians forever well-mannered!

Morne Fortune — historically a fortress; a place of battle hosting the yo-yo dance between the French and the British, with remnants of military presence still dotted around, and now a social hub for locals and tourists alike — our Lucian home, with a most magnificent sunset view, and a house decorated in Moses' yes, proud black and white brickwork signature.

But sadly, the dream was cut short and within days of Moses' collapse, Daddy was gone. I never got to say goodbye and the only goodbye I could hear for years later were his parting words to my mum: "I'll be back." But of course he never was.

In 2017 my mother passed away.

If you've experienced grief, you will know it has a strange way of always shaking things up. What you once knew, becomes no longer, and life takes on new meaning.

That's how I've experienced it anyway.

My mother had suffered months of great physical pain. I was relieved for her when she flew to greater pastures because it had been tough. She had lost her independence, had to experience the 'lesser woman' she had become, and adapting to her 'weaker self' wasn't easy.

However, the strength of who she was, and the contributions she had made to the lives of others shone through her death.

Hundreds of condolence messages from family, friends and all those children she had 'adopted' offered outpourings of love and tears; stories of miracles she had enabled for others blew me away. And as for money, I've never seen so much money placed in sympathy cards!

This was her **legacy**.

Her lovey-dovey.

Her generosity of spirit, kindness and willingness to help others, was being reflected as bright as the rising sun.

It wasn't that Mummy didn't do love, it's that her parental love had a different edge, a learnt behaviour.

Many of my parents' generation behaved the same. My cousins and I, the Patois Girls, laugh out loud hysterically as we recall our crazy parent stories; the no hugs, the no kisses, the strictness. We laugh because although in many ways the experience harsh, our mothers were often 'funny' in their crazy, illogical ways of thinking and methods of dealing with things.

My cousin Maria insists her mother, my mum's sister Titi Edmay, was never that person. It's reassuring to know of course, that there was the other side of love present too.

However, my story is my story and all I can do is reflect and reconsider, to check and change the chapters and transform the scenarios for my healing, my dancing free.

And as I navigated my personal challenges, and past reflections, I reminded myself of *that woman*: 'Mummy', who had made such a positive mark, and contribution to the lives of many.

I reminded myself of who she was, and how she was to be remembered; to not remain stuck in all that she didn't do, and all that she wasn't, the should haves and the better choices she could have made.

I reminded myself of that amazing woman and the loving grandma with a great relationship with all her grandchildren. It was important to maintain balance, to allow for the peace of her soul, as well as the peace, within my heart.

And if it sounds as though I skipped a beat or two and became an angel of delight..

That was not the case.

I wasn't entering into a space of suppression or about to brush past hurts under the carpet. I would continue to listen uncensored to the inner child aggrievements, as and when she chose to show up.

I also knew however, if 'we' were to heal, it was necessary to remain open hearted, compassionate, and to keep love flowing through all channels, clearing stuck debris along the way.

The passing of Moses and Regina resulted in the need of pause and rest within womb-like waters of grief. But despite the heavy sense of loss and endings, I re-emerged each time renewed and with sprinklings of new beginnings.

The Rhythms of **Death** and **Rebirth** come hand in hand.

[Scene Change]

June 2020

The phone rings.

"Pearl, have you got a moment?" asks a friend. "I've got someone here for you, a woman, she is very determined and won't go away!"

"What?"

"Yes, she won't go away and insists I relay this message to you. You may wish to record this…"

She is your mother.

[Black out]

Beaten...

"Were we regularly beaten as children?" I asked my sister Celia.

"No," she responded.

"Are you sure?"

"Yes."

"So why did I tell my therapist I was regularly beaten as a child?!"

My sister laughed out loud at my so-called trauma theory.

"I have no idea. We lived in the same house, we had the occasional slap, or 'licks' as you did in those days, but we were not regularly beaten."

Oh, my goodness, had I just invented a convenient lie? The scenes of that story appeared so real. I was convinced.

What was that all about?

Filters.

Do you know three people can witness the same incident and declare three different stories?

Perception.

It's a matter of perception, isn't it? Based on who you are, your life experiences, belief systems, emotional tendencies… It's as if wearing different spectacles.

I appeared to live in a house of beatings; my sister, not so. The thing is I felt we all experienced this together, but my sister thought me crazy.

My sister and I were on opposite sides of the scale, she on a more 'lyrical' side of life and me, well don't know where I was.

Hmmm… food for thought… now I had to think about what was and indeed what was not true.

I am a fish. Pisces. And as someone with a great interest in the Zodiac Signs and Astrology, I have come to learn that Pisceans are highly sensitive and deeply empathetic individuals. Tell me about it. I feel everything, other people's undisclosed feelings and physical symptoms… don't get me started, it can be so overwhelming at times!

And therefore, childhood instances I remember to be stressful, my sister Celia thinks nothing of. Young Pearl clearly experienced life more painfully, due to her sensitivity susceptibility.

Now. I am not taking away that which appeared real to me, but it is important to acknowledge the potential Pisces traits playing its part within my trauma memory and perceptions.

The 'beaten' film could have been less dark had I known that along the way.

It was SO **healing** and **liberating** to let go.

And then…

Pakatann, Pakatann.

Kwéyòl Etymology

St. Lucian Kwéyòl is a French Creole.

There are various sources of Kwéyòl words as in any language, including African languages, English, Indian languages, Portuguese, etc., but the overwhelming majority of Kwéyòl words derive from French. That is not to say that Kwéyòl is not a unique language — that it is merely a corruption of French. Kwéyòl is a language and deserves to be described as such rather than a variation of something else. To say that Kwéyòl is a dialect and not a language is to show ignorance of the proper, technical meanings of those terms.

Kwéyòl — English Dictionary, St. Lucia Ministry of Education, Issue 2010

Mother-Daughter Healing

"This is a message for Pearl... This much I do know... I am hearing you are Pearl's mum and you want me to relay this message to Pearl."

"Pakatann, Pakatann"

My friend is Jamaican. She doesn't understand those words, but I do.

Under British rule, English became the official language of St. Lucia. Kwéyòl / St. Lucian *Patwa* or *Patois* was discredited and no longer recognised as vernacular, the everyday language of the people. Lucky for me, my parents spoke both English and Kwéyòl within our household.

"Pakatann, Pakatann."

Not hearing, not hearing...

"I need you to speak to me in English please, break it down for me."

My child you are my greatest joy,

you are my greatest joy, joy, joy.

When you were born you were very different to everybody else;

you came out smiling.

I always knew you were going to be trouble,

I never knew how much that smile would trouble me though,

and I love you for it.

I love you Pearl.

In my times of pain, you are my joy,

in my times of struggle, you are my joy,

I just couldn't see it,

I was so blinded with work, with life, with everything, everything that wasn't right,

I spent a lot of my time being unhappy,

I didn't know what it was to be happy,

you did.

I always thought that that happiness would get you in trouble,

because it just wasn't right,

It just wasn't right for anyone to have been as happy as you were.

And child, I just had to 'beat it out of you'.

PAUSE. DID SHE SAY, 'BEAT IT OUT OF YOU?' MY BRAIN IS EXPLODING!!!!

But I was so wrong. I was so wrong.

As I look on you, as I look down at you,

you are still my greatest joy.

And what you have done

what you have done 'my Pearl', my precious…

You have changed my life whilst I am here

You have changed my life 'as' I am here.

And I am always with you.

Sometimes I sit with you on that blue settee,

Sometimes you feel me stroke your hand,

Yes, that's me, that's me…

Sometimes, you feel something in your head, that's me.

Sometimes you feel as if somebody is there,

You can't make it out,

You push out your chest and say, "but wait...?" And then... "nah, nah" (you doubt).

But yes, that's me, that's me.

Oh, my child, oh my Precious Pearl.

Speak to me Pearl, speak to me and tell me,

Tell me that you forgive me,

Tell me that you forgive me.

I've been so wrong.

I can't let you go Pearl.

I'll never let you go.

Oh, you are my precious child.

Thank you

Thank you

Thank you

Amen.

My Heart stops, or so it feels. My head is pounding. I am experiencing a wealth of emotions, shock, incredulity, happiness, wonder… Is this really happening?!!

My friend is a Medium. She is used to 'Spirit' showing up unannounced. But on this day, there couldn't be anything further from her mind.

She tried to ignore it, but the energy was so strong.

She questioned her Guides. "I am so close to Pearl. Am I tapping into the right energy?"

"It is because you are so close to Pearl that you can give her the message the way it is to be given."

"And the beauty is since I've listened," said my friend, "nobody is troubling me, which is great. I can now get on with my house cleaning!"

I sit, winded.

I don't know what to think or what to say.

I am exhausted.

This is mind blowing!!!

I am elated,

I am confused.

This means my mum is present.

I know this to be possible,

I believe in the afterlife and that the soul lives on

but never imagined mummy would show up.

Queen Regina is in the house, (on the blue sofa. Yes, I have a blue sofa)!!

I am happy, yes, I think I am happy...

It's great that she came through for me.

It's great that she felt my heart's need for peace and motherly love.

And wow, so much appreciation gifted from afar

But then...

I feel something murmuring inside.

I get angry.

"Beat it out of you!"

"Beat it out of you!"

She said, beat — it — out — of — you.

There it was.

After all that thinking about whether or not I was beaten?

There it was.

Confirmation.

Pisces sensitive, was beaten!

How could you?!

How could you do that to a child!

It's not fair!

There is no excuse!

That's why I felt so beaten!

It wasn't my imagination!

I AM FURIOUS!!!

You could have made other choices.

What am I supposed to do now?

Forgive you because you have come through from another dimension?!!

You crushed my spirit, crushed what you didn't wish to see!

Get lost.

I don't wish to know!!!!!

I was in a whirlwind.

What do I do with all of this.

The very thing I'd spent so many years reaching towards,

LOVE,

Mothers Love.

Here it was being offered to me;

'Alms of peace' you could say.

It's all I ever wanted and how was I behaving

like a baby throwing its toy out of the pram.

Wise up!

You know better Pearl Jordan.

Do your anger. It's a valid emotion.

But if you wish to heal this relationship, here is your chance.

Do not stay in anger very long.

Remember you believed yourself to have healed quite a lot before this visit.

Remember the whole compassion conversation, and being open to who that amazing woman was and her legacy…? Do you remember that…?

Do you remember all the transformational work you've put yourself through, or were you simply playing lip service?

Get over yourself.

This is a miracle opportunity.

Your mother has brought you a most beautiful, celebratory message of love.

She paints a picture you could never have imagined.

You were a bundle of happiness and joy.

Now you understand why today people repeatedly say: "Pearl Jordan is renowned for bringing, joy, energy and enthusiasm."

It was never beaten out of you!

Your mother may have thought so, but in truth, anything but the truth.

That rhythm of yours,

The essence of who you are,

It continued to pulse.

It may have become dampened,

your shine less bright,

a lingering shadow of deep sadness throughout your life,

but you, Pearl Jordan, are one powerful soul.

There was no stopping that beam of yours.

And now you have the answer to a chapter within your story.

Isn't that great?

Are you going to receive or reject?

Are you willing to expand your forgiveness muscle.

Forgiveness is key, you know this. Here is the real work.

What say you miss humankind, spiritually aware you...?

After my self-talk battering, I decided to put my ego to the side, to see the gift for what it was, and to not only forgive but to give THANKS.

To thank my mother for the expression of pure unconditional love she was able to show from the spirit realm.

To thank her for our reunion.

What a turning point... a powerful one at that!

SHE WAS SCARED

She felt unsafe
She decided
To be fierce, inflexible, impenetrable
She to be feared
There, her rock
Her strength.

She was scared

Possibly felt guilt and shame
She created her armour of defence
You would never see 'her' again
Locked away
Key thrown to the winds
That's her done
Available no more.

She was scared

Wished for more
Hid such thoughts
Now free to share
No more shielding
No more fear
Her spirit of light
Healing hearts alike
Holding her remembrance
Now ever so dear.

Dear Mummy,

Tout bon (St. Lucian Kwéyòl)

All's good

Tout byen (St. Lucian Kwéyòl)

All's well

I Am Blessed

I am **loved**

I am **blessed**

I am on a runaway horse to happiness!

How beautiful… I accepted and received the gift for what it was. Now the mother-daughter healing dance could flow freely between us… Now it was time to allow what I knew in my head to

      drop

          fully

               within

                    my

                        heart

DANCE ALONG

I am blessed

I am blessed

Every day of my life I am blessed

When I wake up in the morning and I lay my head to rest

Every day of my life

I am blessed

I Am Blessed

- Mr. Vegas

[Interlude]

SASSY OAK

Oak, grounded and rooted in her feminine embrace
arms stretched out wide, swirling, dancing with grace
hands on hip, flaunting unabashed, proud
no hiding me,
I stand out loud

Tales of old, tales of new
join me
come close
touch if you dare

Solid...?
Unbending...?
Ha!
Feel my pulse,
vibration drawing you near

Hello
whoosh...
no need to fear
power and strength,
my secrets rooted here

There you go
release, unwind, recline,
I hold you dear

Matriarchal strength
rooted in wisdom years,
the proud Crone in her beauty, glory
cheers!

Thanks for the visit

No, I thank you,
for I move on — energised and gleaming brand new.

Sassy Oak my grounding tree, in Roundwood Park my place of renewed strength and serenity. My stop gap for a chai latte, croissant and nature chit-chat, thanking you for your inspirations that keep me held and on track.

Tree hugs

Blessings   xx

[Lights fade to black]

Act II

THE REHEARSAL

[*overture*]

FAME

Sing–a-long

Baby, look at me and tell me what you see
You ain't seen the best of me yet,
Give me time, I'll make you forget the rest.

I got more in me, and you can set it free.
I can catch the moon in my hand
Don't you know who I am?
Remember my name

Chorus

(Fame)

I'm gonna live forever

I'm gonna learn how to fly

(High)

I feel it coming together

People will see me and cry

(Fame)
I'm gonna make it to heaven
Light up the sky like a flame
(Fame)
I'm gonna live forever
Baby, remember my name...
Remember,
Remember,
Remember,
Remember,
Remember,
Remember...
FAME!

- Irene Cara

[voiceover]

A shift in energy, much needed, Pearl's intuition brings her to Fame.

She jumps from pillar to post, sofa to coffee table, car roof to bonnet (if only... Lol!)

She is in imagination **heaven**!

ACT I releasing, dissipating, allowing her inner child to let loose, foot loose with intoxicating, joyful, rapture.

A well-deserved dance break; she collapses onto a chair and then muses... never mind the magnificent Debbie Allen in the TV series Fame, where she presents a reality check to the performing art students.

Here is how Pearl Jordan, creative director and choreographer does it, in her unique 'stylee'.

ACT 2   THE REHEARSAL   SCENE 1

Day One

[Interior: Shabby walled but clean, large dance studio. Natural light through dusty windows. Rain pattering on roof top. Twenty-one students lounge, some on the floor, some leaning against the walls, others stretching limbs. They are chattering. Enter Pearl Jordan, she sits on a swivel chair, and all fall silent. She has taken to the task of creating a production with a newbie cast. The faces, a mix of excited anticipation, anxiety, even avoidance. Good old first day tension floating through the air...]

Pearl

The *rehearsal* is a journey of self-discovery.

You will experience the good, the bad, the ugly, and the magnificent.

You will be faced with trials and tribulations that challenge all that you thought you knew.

You will be surprised by you, pleasantly or otherwise,

and you will receive many a self-reflection from all angles.

Welcome to the rehearsal space,

A process of personal growth,

and it's through this growth, you will become the artist that shines.

Yes, you are here to enjoy a most wonderful, creative performance experience, but please know, that ultimately you are here to discover who — you — are.

My role is to create a safe space that allows for us all, both you and I, to be held,

held enough to '**dare to go bold**'.

What does this mean...?

In this, our rehearsal space, there are no mistakes,

no failures, only feedback to try something different, to approach from a new angle.

'To play' have fun and to trust that there is magic, your magic, waiting to come through,

to be expressed in your own unique way, providing you remain committed to yourself

and to others — all for one and one for all.

Together we can create great things.

> "No mistakes can be made during rehearsals, only progress toward what works best."
>
> - Jim Jarmusch

And last but not least, the rehearsal is a space of truth — naked truth.

In this environment we drop the pretence, the masks, bravado, all that isn't real.

This is the invitation. Nothing else will do.

If you choose to 'hide', not only will you know it, but we will too.

A space of love and law, comfort and discomfort, where all things lead to 'one'.

Are you ready?

Are you ready to walk this walk, to take those bold steps?

To let go of old limiting beliefs, all the 'I can't'...?

Will you allow in the new, as well as all you already know,

your USP — Uniquely Special Power, Passion, Playfulness, Performance...

Are you ready to commit to the creative process fully

Ready to look in the mirror...?

> "The work of rehearsal is looking for meaning and then making it meaningful."
>
> - Peter Brook

Take a moment, tune into how you feel about all you've heard so far.

What truth or 'lie' sits with you today...?

[End]

Pearl's 'Fame'

You have entered **The Rehearsal**.

Pearl's personal, primal, barefoot foot stomping space, where she dances, rooting into the earth beneath her.

A space where she spirals with the creative process to reveal and re-discover her unique rhythm.

The deep awakening and insights of ACT I motion further clarity and understanding to check those silent, invisible wounds.

With a call to deep dive further into her truth to find meaning, she develops reflective steps that move her closer…

Her performance on the stage of life is at stake

The creative rehearsal process she decides to undertake;

Shining a light, step by step,

Weaving a choreography of unexpected depths,

She dares to go bold in time, energy, space,

To find her healing gold

RHYTHM AND RHYME

Trust in your healing
There is no one pathway
Things may appear disjointed
Unclear
But your healing knows
It knows its best route
To disrobe raw wounds
Layer by layer
One band-aid at a time
Plaster removed
A stitch in time
Saves nine
No need for 'the blues'
Trust in your healing

Jazz on Paper

Life is weird and wonderful, full of surprises; comes at you sideways, takes you unawares, until you realise, *"Ah that's what that was about... That's why it all went pear shaped*... a change in direction. It was a pathway to something greater on the stage of life."

Hard as this can be to accept, there is *always* a gift in everything.

Do you know that? Can you sit with that...?

The next step of my journey was spontaneous and full of surprise themes, ideas, stories, ad hoc 'gifts', experiences unconventional in their order of appearance; clarity appearing in the most unlikely of ways.

The scatter of what showed up how and when, could have been confusing if it weren't for... once a jazz dancer, always a jazz dancer — *'no rhythmic beats too fast for my feet!'*

I danced the dance of all the messages that appeared as part of my journey with flexibility, ease and the occasional two left feet.

Any preconceived idea about how I might heal the callings, the niggles and nudges, was full of twists and turns — stories, poems, dreams, songs, vignettes, and much more appeared in ways I could never have imagined.

It became so '**Now what next...?**' that I likened it to jazz improvisation; a key feature that is uniquely rhythmical, present and passionately ad hoc.

Jazz improvisation can feel scary and unfamiliar. However, the skill is in knowing you have an index of experience and a wealth of knowledge; your muscle memory is grounded in practise, and yours is to trust the 'random' that comes through.

There are no mistakes with jazz improvisation, as there were no mistakes with the order of my journey.

My healing steps were proving to mirror much that I already knew. It's as if the healing dance of life was producing a new hue.

> *"Jazz... it symbolises freedom and empowerment, and a triumph over injustice and oppression."*
>
> - UNESCO, Healing The Wounds Of Slave Trade & Slavery, A Desk Review

Imagine that. Jazz music being recognised within the healing circle of life.

Here was my 'Jazz' on paper.

Ha!

I like that.

I so do.

Now to trust the samples of this novel tune.

ACT 2   THE REHEARSAL   SCENE 3

To be Pearl Willie

***Or not to be*, that is the question.**

Pearl Verna Willie was to be a simple and straight forward name, and it was when in a community of many.

'Willie' a name belonging to the people of Grand Ravine and Gadette, Dennery, St. Lucia, 'a short and stocky people' I was told. My father was born in the district of Dennery, and I remember my grandmother being short and stocky, so that appeared to fit, although my father was tall.

Willie, a nothing unusual name in the Caribbean, but in England a country with its obsession of 'the Willie', it was a different game.

"Next, Pearl Wille"

There was I as always, met with sniggers and giggles at the doctor's surgery.

"Who's calling?"

"Pearl Willie"

"Really… That's an interesting name" Lol!

Laughter at the realm of often a complete stranger when making a phone enquiry.

"Pearl Willie step forward."

Now this is the one. **Audition time**.

I take a deep breath, head held high (not) and I take the step. All eyes upon me, blatantly laughing, how am I supposed to dance and compete for this job if I now feel weakened at the knees?

It's got to go.

I can't stand it anymore.

First opportunity, it **WILL BE GONE**!

It never occurred to me how offensive it must have been for my parents to have me change my name. I didn't even have a conversation about it. I went from Pearl Willie to Pearl Jordan overnight.

Years later my mother with her hands on her hip, in her 'come here let me tell you what I think about you' way, said, "Ms Pearl Jordan or whatever name you are calling yourself...!" And in that moment, the penny dropped, and I knew it must have not been easy for them.

I blamed Equity. Or shall I say, I hid behind Equity, the Performing Arts and Entertainment Trade Union. When you join Equity there is a question of your name, there cannot be two of you... imagine two Beyoncé's? It's never going to happen unless you find that something to make it different, such as a spelling.

Joining Equity was my get out clause.

I eagerly searched for a duplicate of my name within the catalogue. There was no other Pearl Willie, surprise, surprise... but still, I was determined.

I considered Pearl Wylie, close enough, but no, I wanted it gone.

Eventually, I decided on Pearl Jordan. I still can't really remember why, but my mother-in-law's maiden name is Jordan, and perhaps somewhere, somehow, I tried the two and liked the ring of it? Who knows...

Anyway, cowardly, I blamed Equity, its 'essential' name change policy, and left it at that. How could my parents object? Actually, I'm surprised they never did, St. Lucians always speak their mind! But I also happened to mention that 'it was only for dance' and that Pearl Willie was still my name, which it was (phew) on all things official.

But eventually, in 2010 I surreptitiously changed my name by deed poll.

Not even getting married made a difference to that. I have been Pearl Jordan ever since.

What's in a name?

One morning after meditation, I sat with my daily journalling practise, and it occurred to me that *Pearl Willie* might have felt rejected. I know you might think that a strange thing to say because of course I am her, but I suddenly had a sense that I may have upset her. For years she was my identity and then I discarded her, just like that, with animosity, as if she were the enemy. That is not a nice thing to do to a part of you.

I felt the need to make peace, and to ask for her forgiveness.

Self-rejection, it pained me to realise, is not a healthy thing; not in mind, body or spirit. This version of 'self-harm' was to be brought to completion. I can only imagine how on a subtle level this impacted me unawares.

I wrote a love letter to her with much appreciation and grovelled for my misbehaviour!

It's one thing changing your name from a space of positive lightness. It's another because you **chose** to allow yourself to be influenced by others!

I think of Pearl Willie back then, the fact that she didn't have the confidence and sense of self to embody her name and to own it with pride.

I am very aware that I allowed others to get to me, get into my head, under my skin, or you could say, get into my **heart**.

At times though, I did boldly state "Pearl Willie, yes, that's me!" and wouldn't care if a snigger appeared or not. In fact, I willed it. But generally, it became a daily too much.

If only I had more courage… yes, hindsight is a fine thing.

You only know what you know, when you know it.

In St. Lucia when I hear the name 'Willie' I look to the faces, expecting a giggle but nothing, not a hoot of anything. No 'Willie obsession' there, no different from 'Smith' or any regular name.

I also find it interesting how a man can be called 'Willie' short for William without a bat of an eye. As far as I am aware, my brothers also experienced no issues. But a woman...? Laugh to your heart's content.

>Dear Pearl Willie,
>
>It is time to reclaim you.
>
>Am I saying I will now revert back to you?
>
>No. I love the name of my choosing.
>
>But what I won't do is hide from you.
>
>I won't deny you
>
>Reject you my heritage
>
>I celebrate you
>
>I sing out to my roots.

Thank you for showing me how I allowed outside pressures and external environments to interfere with my sense of self, my sense of value.

Thank you for the clear picture of how easy it was to be manipulated back then and how in many ways that has been part of my story.

And thank you. This reflection has allowed me to re-assess the choreography of my life in many ways. It is SO reassuring to confirm that I am certainly **NOT** that person today!!!

The name change came at the start of my career, in my early twenties when entering a new phase of young adult independent life.

The teenage rebel years were over, (not that I ever rebelled against much), so perhaps this was my first attempt of practising that. Perhaps that too was part of the scene.

I felt liberated, but now, due to the circumstances, I understand I was indeed still 'prisoner' to the pain. I hadn't made peace. There was a lot of pretence, and I guess even false bravado within the space.

But now I am free.

Now I welcome a reunion between Pearl Willie and Pearl Jordan.

A match made in Heaven.

You may kiss the bride.

Swanee

It's a Saturday night.

The time is upon us.

I am so **excited**.

I am sitting on the floor, cross legged, in front of the box, aged 6, nose millimetres away from the screen, waiting with bated breath...

And he sings, "Swanee, how I love you, how I love you, my dear ol' Swanee"

There's a chorus of dancers and singers, jazz hands galore. I am in sentient, firework heaven!

Every sway, glide and step pulling me further in towards the telly, and in my imagination, or shall I say, in my heart, I make my way through the screen, my childlike imagination, now part of the scene.

Cake Walk at the ready,

hopping from one foot to the next,

Parasol held high jigging,

can't wait for what's next.

but then.. .a shiver... an unease...

here I am not to be seen...

"This is not for you!!"

I am propelled out of the screen

the end of my childhood lucid dream

The Black and White Minstrel Show

Every Saturday evening, our Caribbean family would huddle around the TV to watch you, light entertainment, on BBC prime-time TV.

White people with blackened shoe polished faces, a regular 'Golliwog' happy, clappy time.

Racist...?

My 6-year-old self didn't think so.

A reflection of me and my family?

How could it be? We didn't blacken our faces with shoe polish.

"No offence meant."

No offence taken.

I can't remember it being deep.

It was the 1960s and 70s, there was entertainer, Sammy Davis Junior; singer, Shirley Bassey; actor, Sydney Poitier, and the sitcom *Love Thy Neighbour*. We black people, without the shoe polish, referred to then as coloured, were represented!

The Late 1980s

Phone call from my agent:

"Pearl, this is a bit of an awkward one, but would you consider lightening up?"

"Lightening up... **I'm confused**."

"Yes, it's just that the other dancer is fair (meaning she was a light skinned black woman), and your dark skin, well the contrast is quite sharp and making it difficult for the lighting of the scene."

"What? Sorry can you repeat that?

I thought I heard you ask if I'd be prepared to *lighten up*.

As in wear lighter make up than my actual skin colour... in order to help with the lighting of the scene?"

"Yes, that's right."

I couldn't fathom what she was saying.

Discombobulated or what!

How could my agent call me to have this conversation without one ounce of awkwardness?!!!

Why did she not stand in my corner and refuse to have the conversation at all?

She seemed so at ease with this request.

What the...?????

My mind was swimming... This cannot be... but it is... surely not... but it is... I want to keep this job... What to do...?

I'd been SO happy to get this gig.

My first TV gig.

Yes. **I made it inside that box!!**

I was so GRATEFUL for the chance to live my dream. Now I was being presented with this!

Between two worlds

There is an enormous divide.

How am I to bridge the gap,

If ever in my life?

It was the late 1980s. The *Black and White Minstrel Show* was done, 1978 had seen the end to that racism (yes, by now, I was innocent no more, knew it for what it was) and yet, here I was, being asked to 'whiten up'. Racism has many shades.

"Um, OK... can I think about it?" said I.

'Sure, get back to me by end of day please".

Can — I — think — about — it?

Can — I — think — about — it.

Tears dripping...

Emotionally thwarted.

Can — I — think — about — it.

Can I...?

I was working as a commercial dancer. I'd already had so many stressful experiences about 'my colour'. I seem to always be one of two or three dark skinned dancers in a room full of hundreds. Every audition brought a triple dose of anxiety: the stress of wanting the job, of remembering and performing the choreography, plus the issue of my colour.

"Will I be the only black person? Is there room for more than one? Will I be too dark skinned? How many fair, light-skinned black girls, closer to white, will there be?

Competition — not of steps, but of skin tone.

Unwanted thoughts dancing in my mind.

The fair skinned were easier to 'blend' — perhaps even pass for white.

But the dark-skinned? There was generally only room for one, if that.

The little girl sitting cross legged inspired by *Swanee* with a craving to be on TV, had had her wish granted, but now it was hanging by a thread.

Your 'choice.'

Did she have a choice...?

"I refused."

After much deliberation, sweating and shaking for fear of losing the job she so wanted and was so enjoying, she said, no. She was prepared to let it go.

I look back at how I made that decision.

I remember feeling how unfair it was.

I remembered how a main concern was the make-up and whether I'd be forced to wear blue eye shadow and weird foundation. Black dancers were always ready for that ongoing fight.

But here I was with a request I could never have imagined, to wear lighter make up to blend with the fairer skinned dancer, and all the other white people in the scene — just for the sake of lighting.

"No. They can find another way. **I refuse!**"

I put the phone down and bawled, so traumatised was I.

And… I am sobbing now.

I am crying for young Pearl who had entered the world of dance full of hope, joy and passion, and who had to deal with the racist culture.

I am weeping because I had no idea this story ran so deep, had no idea there was much healing to be had. I'd suppressed all the pain.

I can feel a niggle, a gut flutter on the left side, the feminine side, highlighting the 'digestion of life' struggles.

And I feel sad.

I feel sad for 'my people'.

I feel sad for all people who have experienced hurt at the hands of racism, discrimination and domination.

It has been very hard replaying this episode… But looking back I am so **HAPPY** I made that decision. Because if I hadn't, I'd feel great shame.

How could I face my young self, had I chosen to go with that racist flow?

I would have had to have gone through a whole process of forgiving myself, loving myself and recognising it for being a different time and seeing it for what it was: unconscious bias, forever the minority, grateful for what you got.

What enabled me to say, no?

How did I find the strength?

How have you found the strength to say no when there is a strong yes to be had?

What was your context?

I was a jazz dancer in the commercial world.

I had already changed my hairstyle to a more European look.

I was wearing make up every day to class (gosh, that make-up thing was hard work!).

I was hanging out in Covent Garden more than I wanted to, in order to fit with 'the in crowd' and the proof was in the pudding. I started to be offered jobs galore and enjoyed being part of the commercial clique.

But now, here I was as if back in the 1970s where people knew no better.

What was the excuse today...?!

Enough already.

I am of strong stock.

My parents, Moses and Regina, never allowed racism and discrimination to diminish their sense of self. They would have risen, 'choops-ed' kissed their teeth and given me a good shaking for showing up on TV 'masked'! That would have been an absolute betrayal to my race and we were not of that age, not anymore.

The buck stops here.

I dug deep and decided to count my losses.

The next day the phone rings.

"The job is still yours. Yes, Pearl. They've said they will find a way."

Stand up for your beliefs

Some you win

Some you lose

The most important thing is you don't 'lose' you.

It's a win, win,

Your win, win.

The Royal Variety Show 1988

"I should be so lucky"

And I felt lucky, lucky, lucky

Six white dancers and… six black dancers!!

What a difference to my previous TV experience.

Dancing with Kylie,

All tones embraced,

Tights dyed in strong coffee to match black skin

I felt so **seen**

Hair, make-up, wardrobe, honouring us all

No 'lighting or lightening' conversations

Pure, utter joy!

In the words of singer Etta James: **at last!**

GOLDEN THREAD

You have a Golden Thread
That 'something' especially yours
The leader of 'your pack'
A driving force.

You have a Golden Thread
For a while you may not know
But she is always with you
Keeping you on the go
Nourishing, nurturing, guiding you on route to your bliss
How she shows up
When she shows up
Make sure you don't miss
The secret is within
Producing your lifetime hit

So, what is your Golden Thread?
That unique thing that belongs only to you
Others may have a version
But not like you.
Yours comes with a 'je ne sais quoi'
A buzzy feeling
A soul food
An 'I can't live without you'.

Your inner guide
That gut message
The nourishment of your life
That if ever paused,
You wander aimlessly as if treading through snow
Until such time you melt into your glow,
Because
Where else would you go?

What is your Golden Thread?
The contribution you make
As if baking a cake
For the world's sake
A constant companion
A given
Your natural high
Your 'inheritance'
Your unique essence
Your Cinderella slipper
Your life's path walking
Forever exploring, growing, shape shifting,

What is your Golden Thread?

ACT 2 THE REHEARSAL SCENE 5

Kimmo

Kimmo was one of the happiest people I ever met.

He wasn't supposed to walk or even live for very long, that was the prognosis given to his mother, my aunt Titi Henrietta, pronounced 'Henritta'. But being the strong black woman she was, she wasn't having any of that!

I remember her making a firm decision and taking determined action as a lioness protecting her young. She, the formidable Henrietta took him off to the Caribbean Sea, "He needs to swim in salt water", said she, convinced of that healing remedy.

On his return from the gorgeous St. Lucia, my child's mind tells me that Kim was walking.

Was it a miracle and indeed, was he actually walking then, who knows? But what I do know is that Kimmo certainly walked, and above all, he danced!

Kimmo was the king of the dance floor. This is where he thrived.

You see, Kimmo was diagnosed with Down Syndrome and in every way based on his limited language — one, two or three words — you wondered how he would communicate and get on in life. But that soon proved to be an unrequited worry.

'Dance is a language of the soul' and Kimmo certainly knew how to move to the beat of his soul.

If you've ever experienced dancing in bliss, or witnessed someone so full of joy, lost in their own world with rhythmic heaven, then there you'd have it. Kimmo sweating, partner swirling, fast foot stepping, intense body, mind, spirit, connection, grooving... That was Kimmo.

And so why an introduction to my beautiful dance battle cousin. "Come on Pollo," referring to my nickname as he joyfully dared me to compete with him on the dance floor.

Whenever I think of Kimmo, I think of the early life lessons learned through his story.

The Power to Decide

My aunt's unwavering hands-on-hips determination and decision making. The way in which she took full responsibility for her son and his welfare.

No was never an option. A **'yes, I can vision'**.

The Power to Face

To overcome the limited outlook, projected towards her son and to move forwards with clear intent.

The Power to Choose and Discern

Despite the opinion of others, my aunt went against the grain and knew from deep within her heart what was best.

The Power to Accept and Tolerate

In life, we can sometimes find it difficult to accept and tolerate that which is different. I learned at an early age that differences are only as different as you choose to make them. They can enhance your experience or swallow you up with comparisons and sense of superiority.

In Kimmo's case, there were no differences. We were all brought up the same. We knew he had Down Syndrome, but that wasn't going to make any difference in any way. He was fully embraced, no more special or different than any of us. In this environment, he was able to thrive.

Joy and happiness

I also witnessed happiness like I've never seen in an individual. No stuff in Kimmo's mind, a simplicity of life that allowed him to be present every day. No noise, nothing extra... most days he could be found playing his favourite music, choosing his vinyl records with expertise.

Music, dance and being 'full up' were his pleasures of the day.

"How are you Kimmo? Have you had enough to eat?"

"I'm full up, right to the top," would be his response as he gestured with a flat hand under his chin, depicting a rise from way on down, up to as far as he could go.

It is fair to say that Kimmo was full up with happiness and the abundance of life. He was fully supported, encouraged, celebrated and ultimately loved, beyond measure.

Independence whilst interdependent

Kimmo was able to live life independently. He was coached to travel solo by public transport, to go to the shops, and to work. And he holidayed. He was always traveling somewhere with a group. His life was rich in so many ways.

OK. So now I hear the question, "Wouldn't you be happy if you lived such a life without responsibility and stress free 'to do' lists? Wouldn't you be happy if you didn't have to navigate relationships and work demands, etc, etc?"

Yes, I hear you and certainly I would be.

But the consideration is this: might it be possible to bring that sense of rhythm into your life, despite all the challenges and such?

What if you chose to breathe into life more easily?

What if you had the determination to live a 'simply being happy' life?

How might that influence how you show up and isn't it worth exploring to see what it might bring?

Imagine providing that space for yourself and for others, both on a personal and professional level? Perhaps you already do.

The invitation is, how can you follow in Kimmo's footsteps and be 'full up, right up to here?'

And if you don't know, what could be a first step?

> *"Dance is a hidden language of the Soul."*
>
> - Martha Graham

ACT 2 THE REHEARSAL SCENE 6

Pearlicious Cake - A Little Story...

Pearlicious

not to be mistaken with 'pernicious', was delicious.

And she wanted to bring her delish-self out into the world, so she chose two delicious souls to help her experience this earth.

She sparkled and beamed with wondrous delight, she skipped and hopped, enchanted with life. Having tea and cake were her favourite game, what more could she want, so much happiness gained.

Along the way, Pearlicious started to feel not so delicious after all, more tasteless to be true, so Pearlicious hid her delish-self, cocooned under a stool.

And because the light didn't shine much where she sat, it became increasingly dark and matter of fact.

Cocoon
no butterfly at my door,
Caterpillar state
hungry to radiate
trapped by a 'no sell by date'.

Until one day...

"**Crumbs**, crumbs, cake crumbs for sale, for you my dear one, pick up the trail."

"Cake. Did someone say **cake**?" Her ears picked up. Perhaps it was now worth stepping out.

So out she came, at first still fearful and bound, holding her Cocoon closely for safety all year round.

But in time she grew to learn the world was not such a dark place after all, so she skipped and hopped enchanted with life once more.

Cocoon forgotten, until a knock at her door.

"Hello. Do you remember me? I am your friend the cocoon. You brought me to life to shield and protect you. I've been with you committed for a very long time. But now it appears you are ready to fly. May I remind you of our song?

Cocoon
no butterfly at my door
Caterpillar state
hungry to radiate
trapped by a 'no sell by date'."

"Oh, *Cocoon*," said Pearlicious, "I'm ever so sorry. Do come in. You're right. I totally forgot.

I always knew there was something hanging around, as if a shadow, a feeling that would only allow, one step forwards, two steps back, not too far now, pulling back.

Now I know that that was you, holding me tight with **loving glue**.

I thank you for doing such a great job, but now it is time to turn things around... Oh no, no, no, please don't sob!!"

They hugged and wept and hugged and wept as they recalled how it was, they first met.

Wiping the tears, Pearlicious exclaimed, "I know what, let's have tea and cake, our once upon a time game!"

They ate and they talked, enjoying every slab and slurp, until it was time to decide what next without any hurts.

"Cocoon," said Pearlicious, "I love you dearly for having been such a dear friend. What a protective role you played."

"When I called upon you. I was innocent and young, full of stress, worry, depleted of fun. But today, I am ready to run, to fly kite high as far as the Sun.

No more intense fear and darkness for me. It is time to paraglide with life and be full of Glee."

"But that wasn't the agreement!" Cocoon stamped defiantly.

"You created me and said, 'hide me', so I took you to the moon and there we stayed avoiding all that gloom."

"Oh, dear…" said Pearlicious apologetically.

"Way back then. I forgot to say, that together we stay until darkness fades into the light of day.

As I have grown older, I realise that life is forever changing, nothing is ever still, time really does heal.

I didn't tell you this before because I didn't know it at the time. And I'd forgotten about our pact, our 'no sell by date', so didn't share this with you, as I came to realise.

I am so sorry, let's decide what next, because the deal of old no longer accepts.

Cocoon, you can be free to live a new life, to no longer be attached to me.

Surely that's worth considering. Both of us able to do as we please?

We made a pact that was made in fear, can't hold onto that forever, and thankfully happier times are bidding us near.

Time to **laugh**, to **sparkle** and **beam**, tell you what, let's transform this and see.

What say you Cocoon, what say you...?"

SOS

When the going gets tough
In need of clarity and soul-utions
Stand back. Observe. Steer.
Take a pause
Relax
Retreat into silence
Let stillness be your guide
Tune in to your inner eye

Is there a learning to be had
A reflection of you
Are you ready to acknowledge your part
Or too blind to see the view

Stand back. Observe. Steer.

When clarity demands a first step
Even though it be a dark moon
Know it will wax into the light
Of a shiny, silvery moon

Commune with nature

Exercise

Journal

Draw

Paint

Sing

Dance

Bake

They shift your grace
Allow for space
A bird's eye view enhanced

You may have an SOS practise
If so, do share
You never know who might be hiding
Under a darkened stair.

ACT 2 — THE REHEARSAL — SCENE 7

Dancing with the Smell of Fear

One day, I allowed myself, very much unwillingly, to go to a space of such deep-rooted fear, resistance and ugliness, such darkness that I thought I might combust if I dared...

That's if I **dared**...

Tears streaming, blubbering, ugly cry tears, a cascading flow of childhood fears, anger, unworthiness, undeserving, unlovable tears

Dare I? Don't I? Go there?

Dare I? Don't I show up here?

Uncontrollable, a force so strong, gut wretched, twisted, and mangled,

Ahhhhhhhhhhhhhh!

Can I? **Can I dare ...?**

Every pore releasing from roots deep within my soul womb,

Stomach cramping, my body revolting, a reminder of my youthful monthly cycle tears...**too much to digest!**

Old parts shedding,

bleeding

The past releasing

Shifting...

rotten, unrecognisable fears

dancing a tango so closely, at one with the smell of...

death, it feels so...

I don't think I will survive

Dare I? don't I? go there?

dare I? don't I show up here?

useless, waste of space, who am I kidding?

dark, dark despair

every cell whizzing, tumbling, bumping

too deep, too deep, too...

I hear a guttural cry, "Help!" Rooted as if from depths of the earth.

every sentient cell of my being screaming,

petrified,

begging for a healthy destiny,

gravel sob, sobbing

And then...

And then... **sunset**.

Is it?

As if by magic, the most beautiful sunset ever seen in Willesden Green.

I stop, squint and stare through a haze of tears, perplexed at its wonder, its drawing me hypnotically near

A magnetic appreciation too powerful to ignore, suddenly raising my vibration to a heightened awareness of…

… I hear a whisper: "Choice".

My eyes whizz right to left, left to right

"Yes, choice… *even in the darkest hour you have choice, up, down, forwards, back, side to side; what do you choose now, today?*"

Well, I certainly wasn't expecting that.

I wipe my tears and snotty lips

What now…? Retch or receive?

Hmmm…

One of those crossroad 'power' moments …

Power to Face
Power to Accept
Power to Let Go

An invitation to self-victory.

I move to the window, open it to fully immerse and absorb the orange, red, golden, shape shifting glow and spell binding light

Mother.

Nature.

Nurture.

How could I not receive…?

I wise up, in a gentle, *'pick yourself up and dust yourself down'* way.

Magical Magnificence

Shorter breaths, less gulping, more at peace, exhausted, but now lost in the awe of the gift of this time.

The symbolism ever so clear.

Birth. Death. Rebirth, the option is here...

Every sunset brings a new dawn, a new choice, new opportunity for new possibilities.

A chance to let go of the old and welcome in the new.

To let **die** and be **reborn**.

Huh,

Little broken me. Not so broken now after all.

I inhale and exhale into the beautiful silent, vibrant vision of golden, red light and trust that tomorrow brings a fresh — refresh — reset.

gunk released

old stuff percolating no more

volcanic emotional eruption done

the dark night of the soul, over.

Sleep...

...I awake to the gift of a new day.

I am still alive!

Well, I never.

Delicate, but I feel a rising heat within my heart.

Tingles sparking in other bodily parts.

There, there, sweet one, little one

You did it

We did it

We danced through the smell of fear

And now,

Grace...

"What we are today, come from our thoughts of yesterday
And our present thoughts build our life of tomorrow
Our life is the creation of our mind."
- Buddha

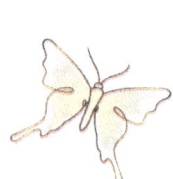

My Body is My Temple

Suitcases at the ready.

Children happy and excited.

Passports?

Check

Supper-efficient, proud and organised a day in advance?

Check, check

One nights more sleep.

Family holiday at the ready?

Big time check!

And then...

You have got to be kidding me!

How is this possible?

I can't move.

What?

I can't move!

Every part of me screams out in pain as I attempt to move.

It's not going to happen.

My back is behaving as if it's been electrocuted by lightning.

There is no give. I am shocked into stillness and to add to it all a cough has appeared with every spurt adding to the pain.

I have no idea what I did or what happened.

I was fit and now I am not.

Holiday over.

MY BODY IS MY TEMPLE

*She never fails me
in her wisdom she shows up
every time
with kindness and love
she reflects my inner mirror
making it clear that change is the only option
a required change I never saw coming.*

*My body is my temple
she never fails me
in her wisdom she makes herself known
she nurtures my soul
nudging me back to health.*

*With love
with care
with consideration
compassion
she will collude with me only so far
waiting patiently, oh so patiently, for the love of time*

that time

Directing me to put right the wrong
to sort my thinking
sort my feelings
to acknowledge the hurts that reside deep inside
rising to the surface
specific in her placement
message loud and clear
silent no more

My body
she is truly my temple
she never fails me
sees me as if in
I C U
Intensive Care Union
in her wisdom she states

No more.

Pain

I was in such **excruciating** pain that a visit to A&E was a must. I cried out as I attempted to leave the bed to make it down the stairs. I literally had to put my back against the wall and slither along until I made it to the front door. This slithering was to play a huge part in mobility over the next couple of days.

Tests proved inconclusive. I returned home with painkillers.

Why and how had this happened? I kept on asking myself.

How did I hurt my back? None of this made any sense. And as for the non-diagnosis, I felt completely in the dark.

I made my way home, slithered back up the stairs, along the wall, and back into bed, wincing and 'ouching' all the way.

It was Easter weekend. My Homeopath was away. I was a student of Homeopathy. It was over to me to self-prescribe, that's if I could distance myself enough away from the pain.

I asked my husband to grab specific remedies for muscle ache and pain. I kept on chopping and changing desperately praying I'd hit the pain spot.

Nothing.

A day later, I finally, woke up.

"Right, Pearl Jordan. What you're doing is focusing only on the part of your body that's experiencing the pain and trauma. You are not working or thinking as a Homeopath. Remember, Homeopathy is a holistic approach to health and well-being and therefore you need a holistic approach to your recovery, mental-emotional, physical and spiritual.

What would you do if a patient came to you with a similar situation? You would put your detective Columbo hat on, and ask what happened before your back seized... *wouldn't you?*

You'd ask them all about the symptoms, what makes it worse, better, how it is experienced at different times of day, any 'strange, rare or peculiar' symptoms? All that kind of enquiry to help identify a 'like for like' remedy that matches your complaint.

But instead, what are you doing? Grabbing aimlessly at different remedies in the hope that one works. You know there are hundreds of back pain remedies, and the work is to narrow things down... There really is no avoiding the effort that it takes.

What happened before your back seized?

I was running around, packing, getting all things ready to leave the following day.

Did you feel any strain or such at any time?

No.

What was going on in your life prior to packing?

Like what...? I questioned myself.

What was going on in your life before all the packing activities and holiday prep?

Hmmm...ah... yes... now you are talking... **Lesson time**.

"It's important to realise that our body is a product of our thoughts. We are beginning to understand in medical science the degree to which the nature of our thoughts and emotions actually determines the physical substance and structure and function of our bodies."

- Dr John Hagelin, Quantum Physicist

The Mind-Body Connection

I had been in overwhelm, juggling far too much, and I would not allow myself to stop long enough to rest and replenish. (Sounds familiar...?)

I was also in my early forties and peri menopausal, a space of mega hormonal change; that under-represented space of contemplation and truth re-consideration...

Who are you now?
Where is your **self-nurture** and **nourishment**?
What are you creating for *yourself* not everyone else?

The body, in her wisdom, will keep going for as long as she can until it is time to 'break' and that break can manifest in many forms.

In homeopathy we refer to this as a process of discharge, a release, for example a cold, flu, an abscess... back pain.

When in busy bee mode, you can avoid, leaving no space for the health truth to unfold.

The stress hormones adrenaline and cortisol feed the system and keep you going until such time...it is time.

I once heard the build of stress hormones referred to as acid building in your body's system. An acid state is an unhealthy state. The body in health needs to be more alkaline.

The acid/alkaline condition depends on the foods you eat, the environments you are exposed to and, of course, your thoughts and feelings.

We all understand we have an immune system, and the aim is to keep it strong (alkaline); a weakened system (acidic) weakens the body.

Imagine a fizzy drink with a slow build. At some point that fizz will pop.

In the case of the body, often that pop occurs when a 'gap' appears.

I am not sure if you are aware of this or have experienced it as such, but if working in a highly stressful job for example, once on holiday you can experience a cold, flu, skin rash, a fall?

That is your form of 'fizzing through the gap'. This is your body telling you how much you did not rest and recoup beforehand.

In my case, I didn't even get to the holiday. Clearly with all the excitement about enjoying a well-deserved break, my body thought me already there.

It must have been in such a relief and 'at last' state that it couldn't contain itself.

All the checking of passports and suitcases at the ready suggested time to let go.

At last it could give way, drop all that I had been holding onto.

AND at last, because my body loved me so, it would make certain that the area of concern would direct me to my healing, in mind, body and soul.

If a flu or cold, this would suggest build your immune system, keep it strong daily with healthy foods, water, supplements, rest, etc.

In my case, the lesson was to be much deeper.

In the past I had experienced burn out, not once, but twice. Burn out is when your nervous system becomes 'shot' and completely breaks down, it crumbles with a clear message of "STOP!" In both cases I became bedridden for weeks.

The first experience occurred in my twenties literally in the 'wings' off stage.

My life was one of juggling my performance arts degree, teaching, dancing, creating productions. I was forever on the go (Fame!)

One day the WAC company I belonged to called FUSION, we left the stage to a resounding stamping of feet and the shouts of encore. Back on we went and gave a final blast of a performance. But once back in the wings, I started to cry and shake and laugh and shake and cry and shake... a visit to the doctor confirmed burn out.

The second burn out... performance, teaching, plus children, house and home. I was wise to the symptoms and put myself to bed.

This time however, clearly due to not having learned the lessons of the past, now the body in its wisdom was stating "no more".

It took a while for me to come to grips with this, in between the cries of the pain, but hang on in there I did, until slowly, slowly, the answers started to creep in.

Once I had wised up to what was going on, I knew exactly the homeopathic remedy to self-prescribe.

What was the magical remedy?

I could name it, but that would be doing you a disservice.

If you find yourself in this juggling overload twist, you may indeed benefit from Homeopathy, but the remedy would differ from mine.

The one I chose covered my specific mental-emotional, physical and spiritual state, past and present.

It was for my unique situation — like for like.

Your remedy would match your unique circumstances and symptoms.

Although often dis-ease can sound the same, it never is, your flu is not my flu. My back pain is not yours.

The Gift of this Time

The remedy worked like magic, literally shifting my symptoms within hours, enough so I could start to move.

By day three I was ready to jump out of bed and get a moving and a grooving, but I did not.

I decided to further honour this getting to know you time with my body, to connect with it more deeply.

I came across the Polynesian Ho'oponopono healing mantra:

I'm sorry
Please forgive me
I thank you
I love you

And recited this throughout, making peace with my body, with the decisions I had made, making peace with life.

I showered my body with love and gratitude for this chance to heal all invisible stress' and trauma I had been holding within my body.

I journalled, writing about the juggling, all the stress in need of releasing and how I would do so. AND I made a pledge to never return here again.

Deep in my bones I made a firm decision that I would make resting, taking time out to refuel and facing the stresses of life head on, a ubiquitous priority. I deserved to remain in the mind body spirit wealth of health.

And one last thing, the beauty of this time, the gift of gifts presented to me was the mind-body connection passion it awoke within.

I had always been highly interested in the psychology of Homeopathy, but this experience truly brought it home. I started reading all that there was to read and collated a library of mind-body books.

This is now a central part of my health and wellbeing coaching practice.

It never ceases to amaze me what this knowledge brings to clients. It changes lives and runs so deep.

It helps individuals to see how much the past impacts the present.

How the body is a container of all that has been shut down and suppressed over the years.

It also shows you when the time is right to heal.

There is no straight timeline.

When you are 'ready', when your innate wisdom knows that you have the strength to 'deal'.

When your body decides to collude with you no more, it will show you the most clear and direct path to equilibrium. It could be stubbing your toe repeatedly or in my case back pain, not one-sided pain but the whole torso to consider.

There is so much intelligence at play. It's a wonder..

As Louise L. Hay states in her book *You Can Heal Your Life*:

The Back

Represents the support of life.
Affirmation: *I know that Life always supports me.*

Muscles

Represents resistance to new experiences… our ability to move in life.
Affirmation: *I experience life as a joyous dance.*

The irony of me having to be reminded to enjoy life as a joyous dance!

YOUR BODY IS YOUR TEMPLE

She never fails you
in her wisdom she shows up
every time
with kindness and love
She reflects your inner mirror
making it clear that change is the only option
a required change you never saw coming.

In her wisdom she states:

"No more."

FORGIVENESS

I forgive myself
I forgive my past

I behaved as I did
Said what I said
Felt what I felt
Danced as I danced
Based on what I had
The rhythms available to me at the time

Today I am wiser
Am renewed in many ways
And so...

I forgive myself
I forgive my past

I behave as I do

Say what I say

Feel what I feel

Dance as I dance

Based on what I have

The rhythms available on this present day.

I let go of the illusions of self-judgement and shame

I choose self-love over fear any day

I am doing my best

Give yourself a break!

I forgive myself

I forgive my past

I am grateful for the 'gifts'

Provided all the way.

ACT 2   THE REHEARSAL   SCENE 9

Permission to Go Solo

I am standing in the wings, and I am freaking out. Performance anxiety is very unkind. I am so nervous. I can't begin to tell you how much I am shaking inside.

It didn't matter I had rehearsed and knew what to do, a complete focus on all that may go wrong, so outside looking in, and worrying about what people might think, say, and the potential criticism coming my way.

It would have been great if my mind was keen on simply having a good time.

So lost in my head… **Am I enough…? Do I have what it takes?**

I had no sense of 'we' all of us in this together, audience, production team, fellow dancers, all rooting together, wanting the best. It was all about 'me', self-obsessed.

If only I was more in the joy of the present moment and not so focussed on a future of ill gains.

I take a deep breath, the musical cue begins, I count 5, 6, 7, 8, and on I go…

I dance my steps into the light. I am giving the audience my everything, jazz hands reaching in every direction, but something didn't feel quite right.

For goodness sakes, in such a panic was I, I was dancing as if my eyes were closed and partly, they were!

I opened my gaze fully… Where is the audience…? They are nowhere to be seen.

Think pantomime… the question, *"Where are they…?"* and the call response, *"They're behind you!!!"* That was me, facing upstage, away from the audience, towards the cyclorama screen, my back in jazzy action, my front not to be seen.

Once I realised, and before I could faint with embarrassment, my instinct kicked in and I danced, I danced a performance of a lifetime, as if I'd been given a solo spot. I improvised with such gusto and confidence, whilst keeping an eye on the other dancers until such time I was back on beat and in tune with the routine.

When I came off stage, I was a shaking wreck, so nervous was I about the onslaught of comments and feedback I was about to receive. In fact, so stressed and traumatised was I, that I couldn't even remember the comments, it became one big blur!!

For several weeks I replayed the trauma in my mind but then slowly I started to see the scene in a new light…

Did I run off stage and hide?

Did I 'corpse' and die on stage, or did I do the best that I could all things considered?

Over the years I have reflected on this story, this **very** story that inspired the 'Fame' director speech of ACT II Scene 2.

There is a gift in everything, (a repeated theme throughout the book) and pleased to say, as always, so it proved…

I came to realise that something magical had happened on that day. Despite my brain sizzling in panic, I continued to dance. I didn't run off stage. I didn't freeze. I danced. I danced as they say, 'like no one was watching'.

I improvised as if it were a solo moment. The audience would never know that it was never set. Yes, the performers, director, choreographer, the team will know, but the audience will be none the wiser.

That is when I gave myself **'permission to go solo'**.

Solo...

As a professional, you could say, well of course you danced, that's obvious, the show must go on. But the point is this:

When I lost myself in my 'solo' moment, although heightened with anxiety, and certainly with an extra boost of fight of flight adrenaline, I entered a space of performance equilibrium. It's the best way I can describe it; a space of self-dependency, a self-trust that I did not know I had. It is as if I 'leaned' into me.

The more I reflected on things, the more my self-confidence grew, and the less overwhelmed I became with performance anxiety.

What was it that allowed me to go solo?

> *"I stole from everything I ever heard, but mostly I stole from the horns."*
>
> - Ella Fitzgerald, 'Queen of Jazz'.

I stole from everything I had ever danced, every step I'd ever created, every presentation I'd ever spoken, every production I'd ever directed. This wealth of experience I had 'in the bag'. It is this, I came to realise, and more that fired up my dance within, providing the steps to my success. My solo was on the shoulders of practice, practice, many a practice, and all that came before.

Have you found yourself in situations riddled with anxiety so much so, it feels like a stomp pounding in your head... your heart...? The tension being so intense it's all you can do to not vibrate and bounce across the floor.

If you don't know what I am talking about, congratulations. I bow to your healthy grounding.

But if you do, what would happen if in that moment you remembered all that you have in the bag?

What would happen if you stole from every presentation, or board room conversation, every moment on stage or whatever the circumstances, what if you reminded yourself of your history, your backlog of experience, skills and abilities... What would that bring?

And what if you called upon all things at that moment of stress? What if you allowed yourself permission to go solo, to tap into the wealth of your inner knowing, trusting that exactly what you need will show up for you in that given time?

What if...?

I admit this can be scary. But having been through the process many a time, both personally and through helping other people overcome their performance and presentation fears... You are worth it... It is worth it for the FREEDOM that it brings.

Worth it for the getting to know yourself.

Worth it for the **creativity** and **innovation** that suddenly appears.

Only recently I was online teaching a movement-inspired session and the music wouldn't come through so what to do...? Quick as a flash, a nursery rhyme dropped into my mind, I taught it to the group and we laughed and we danced.

That is what permission to go solo brings. It teaches you be free, to explore in whatever way shows up. It is amazing what you learn about yourself and your ability to flex and flow. And this is not limited to performance, this is available to you every day of your life.

One more note... if you dare to explore this solo invitation, remember:

"Do not fear mistakes — there are none."
- Miles Davis

F.E.A.R

False. Expectations. Appearing. Real
False. Evidence. Appearing. Real
Face. Everything. And. Rise.

Fear in its many guises and limiting-belief costume changes

Twinned with 'safety', a perfect pair

You believe more in what you 'can't, than you 'can' and either way, you are right

You lack the confidence or courage to 'face'

You create worst case scenarios in your mind

You may even avoid the silence it takes

To find the answers deep inside

As for going against the grain

To stand out loud

Dancing to the tune of others for so long

You've forgotten to hand back the baton

*'Love is what we were born with,
fear is what we have learned here.'*
- Marianne Williamson

Rivers run deep

Mountains high

You dear one

Are destined to **FLY**...

First   Love   Yourself

Bullies Ballerinas

I'm in a room of young Arts Management Candidates, all with aspirations of being a leader within the arts sector. We are invited to imagine a project we may wish to create or lead on, the idea being that we explore all areas, the who, how, why, what, when, SMART Goals, pros and cons. We put ourselves in the arts manager role.

I suddenly feel the corners of my lips rise and my eyes begin to twinkle. I know exactly the project: my jazz dance company, a longtime dream!

My mind starts to spin with wonder. I list all the company members, the best jazz dancers and teachers I have had the privilege to work with.

I list all the styles I have experienced and the history and knowledge I'd accumulated over the years, readily available to teach and to freely share.

I imagine the energy of all the musicals and artists that had inspired me as a child; *West Side Story, On the Town*, Gene Kelly, all things Fred Astaire and Ginger Rogers, Cyd Charisse, Dorothy Dandridge, Carmen Jones…I called on the energy and spirits of all those inspirations and almost danced myself off the page as I planned!

This was to be a first UK company of its kind, and I was so excited at the prospect of giving birth to her. 'Jazz dance accessible to all' would be her imprint, her Golden Thread. I could feel the company so strongly in my gut. Pictured her so clearly. 'She' was a given.

I listened to a young man's story, the idea of a community choir. Soon I saw him and his choir on TV. They are now renowned, singing in their glory on various channels. He and his vision are now of VIP status.

As for my vision, my toe-tapping, finger-clicking, feel-it-in-my-gut jazz dance company, I left the arts management course full of conviction, encouraged by the enthusiastic responses received and then… nothing.

Zero attention and action.

How could I have had such a strong, clear feeling, and yet do nothing…? I mean, really, how was that possible? How could an idea feel so alive and then deflate to a shrivelled nothingness? In the moment, I felt the company so deeply in my bones and truly believed in 'her' and yet…

If you've ever been in that space, you'll understand how frustrated and confused I felt. And even more scary was how uncertain I began to feel about 'me'.

Who was 'that' person who could be so certain, so inspired by her ideas, who could have such clarity but then let it go as easily as it came?

Was it just a game or did I truly believe?

VIGNETTE

I felt a tingle in my fingers and a tingle in my feet,
The rhythm of life produced such a powerful beat
I may have felt pulled to step right back
but now I was certainly back on track!

Inspired by song The Rhythm Of Life

- Dorothy Fields

- Cy Coleman

Goodbye to Moses

When my dad Moses suddenly passed away in 1993, it was understandably a huge shock, and for months I lived life as if in a slow lane, a dream-like state.

I remember the stress around having to view his body, should I, shouldn't I? Surely it made sense to hold onto the healthy, vital image I had in mind rather than the collapsed version so clearly defined. I was stressed with a capital 'S' and, although I chose to view his body and it proved to be not that big a deal, my psyche was shattered, trauma instilled.

I continued to audition for dance roles, but neither my head nor heart had interest.

I couldn't shake off a feeling of 'empty' and mentioned this to prominent stage and tv actress Ann Mitchell, whose post graduate acting course I was attending at WAC.

As I remember it, there was a lot of 'psychology' in the acting space she held, a method that helped us to dive more deeply character wise, so I am not surprised my struggles rose to the surface.

Ann, who is now a dear friend, explained I was experiencing the effects of grief. I had no idea.

I thought grief was about sadness. I didn't know it could show up as your head in the clouds 24/7. Thank goodness for that turning point.

And another fellow student added:

"You are experiencing trauma, that's what it does, slows things right down. And yes, grief is trauma, it's just that we don't often see it that way."

Trauma?? Grief is **trauma**...?? So that's what it does...?

It was time to accept the reason for my numb state.

I had worked so hard to 'be known in the biz', to be of the jazz dance in-crowd. I was receiving invitations from directors and choreographers, having private auditions; I was in dancer flow. It was so lovely to be in that space at last.

But a wise friend said, "Do grief now Pearl, don't wait to be at a bus stop in five years' time and suddenly start bawling your eyes out. It **will** catch up with you. There is no side-stepping the grief blues."

And so, taking heed, I chose to pause and move away. None of it, lights, camera, action, appeared that important now anyway.

I tried to do the 'grief thing' alone but in the end, it was clear I needed bereavement counselling. I'd never experienced counselling before, thought I'd speak about my father's death, get rid of the sadness and start living again.

Instead, I was introduced to my inner child. I didn't even know she existed.

The 'inner child' archetype is attributed to Psychologist and Psychiatrist Carl Jung.

My understanding is that the inner child is believed to be a subpersonality part of you in adulthood that reflects your childhood experiences, behaviours and emotions.

All that you learned as a child before puberty could be the driver for that which you struggle with today.

The bereavement counsellor offered:

"You may well be playing out the pain of your inner child. Get to know her, take her out for walks, ask her what she wants, allow her voice."

Gosh, imagine that. Not only did I have an inner child in need of attention but to take her out…?

As crazy as it sounded, I was open to giving her a chance. I would try anything to transform the space I was in. And boy, did **she** have much to say…

Childhood this and childhood that, disgruntled this and disgruntled that, dance experience this, dance shut down that, a kaleidoscope of once suppressed stories!

She was on a roll. But then came the gold... A beautiful message of hope received, one day, during a meditation and journalling reprise.

"You will reach a waterfall of clear prism rainbow light, and the grief of gold will be yours to ignite."

It sounded poetic and full of potential, but what did it truly mean...?

In my culture death is not a taboo.

People wail, speak openly about it, children are included in all aspects of death and funerals. We view dead bodies. We pray, eat, drink, tell stories, dance and celebrate. We get over it and continue with life.

This was the ease of my experience of death and dying, so to go through such emotional turmoil was very surprising.

Why could I just not get over it as I'd witnessed on many an occasion?

It was the closeness.

This was my **dad**.

On the night I heard of Daddy's death, I had been at the theatre, laughing hysterically at one of the funniest productions I had ever seen. My friend Jeanefer said she had heard of Moses' death, but it was clear that I was none the wiser. She thought it best to wait until the end of the show to tell me. I don't think she actually did the telling. I can't remember the who did the telling. The trauma had already set in.

One minute I was full of joy, the next, it was catapulted from me.

The description of my dad's fate was such that I wished him peace. I knew the man he was, would hate every breathing moment of the non-communicative stroke victim he had become. I prayed for his release because it was clear there was to be no full recovery, no quality of life.

My dad needed to be his jovial, functioning self on the other side. And he was. That I knew for sure. He 'made it clear' a number of times.

When he died, I didn't realise he would remain forever present...

Moses appeared to grandchildren, whispered hello in my son Michael's ear... was seen at my sister's wedding and aided a reluctant grandson at the time of his birth.

One day in great detail, my nephew innocently pointed to a photo and said, that's the grandad who helped me when I was being born. His story matched his mother's memory of her caesarean and its complications in every detail. You can imagine her shock especially as Moses had 'left the body' many years before his grandson's birth.

The story described a dance between my nephew in utero not ready to be born, and Moses encouraging him to do so.

Aww how lovely. No missing out for Moses. Forever nearby. Forever present.

It's so heartwarming and reassuring to have the idea of life after death affirmed. Perhaps if I'd recognised this more at the time, it would have greatly eased the grief of mine.

But then came, another golden nugget.

Do you remember that jazz dance company dream? The one that slept in a dark drawer somewhere?

She began to stir...

Bullies Reborn

My friend Jeanefer and I began teaching together on a more regular basis.

Our friendship went back as far as primary school and we had danced side by side throughout our lives: secondary school, WAC Weekend Arts College, Middlesex University (then Polytechnic). We had held numerous conversations about one day having a dance company specialising in all the styles we had encountered and loved.

Our mutual thoughts reflected the jazz dance company idea of old. So clear were we, we arranged for a photo shoot, created a brochure and shared our ideas with leaders in dance. It was a matter of time...

An invitation arrived from the Northeast of England to help rejuvenate community dance within the Newcastle area.

Such a success was the dynamic duo, the 'Pearl and Jean show' and ever-increasing demand for more public workshops and weekly school dance residencies, that we were obliged to pause for a second.

What now?

Could this be it?

I felt the commercial dance career fading.

Since my dad's death, I hadn't fully re-immersed into that world. It felt too stressful. It took so much energy to 'play the game' and I was no longer the same. Grief had made sure of that.

The commercial world of dance began to feel fickle. I started to question my contribution.

There is a lot of good to be said about the world of entertainment but that version of dancer in me was beginning to fade.

What did I offer? What difference was I making?

In relation to my partnership with Jeanefer and the change we were making to people's lives, the joy of dance we were witnessing through the hearts of those we taught and created with. In the scheme of things, one outshone the other.

I now had purpose as well as passion.

Life. Death. Rebirth

Endings and Beginnings.

A theme that would reoccur again and again over the years.

I asked myself:

What do you **lose** by saying 'no' to the old?

What do you have to **gain** by saying 'yes' to the new?

These 'no', 'yes' prompts I always use. I find they place me straight to the heart of the matter, brings clarity, peace of mind and spurs you into action.

It is such an amazing consideration for insight.

Here was my clarity:

No unnecessary make up, hair masks

No jumping to someone else's tasks

Yes, to being in my own powerful right

Yes, to an adventure of new life

Here was the golden nugget.

I had reached my *'waterfall of clear prism rainbow light, and the grief of gold was now mine to ignite'*.

Oh, the power of dance

it heals me so

forever in my corner

the showstopper

I have come to know

Bullies Ballerinas Dance Company was Born

A silly name I know, it came from a joke. We were certainly not bullies or ballerinas plus there was an association to a footballer, (told you it was silly) but it made us laugh out loud and so we thought, why not!

Jeanefer and I invited the crème de la crème of our dancer friends to join us on the ride of the ever-growing company.

We offered every possible jazz dance style and contemporary modern dance too, but it got to a point where we had to ask, "Who are you? Are you going to provide everything just because you can or is it time to niche into your jazz brand?"

We let go of the contemporary modern and honoured the dream that had always been. A one hundred percent jazz dance company committed not only to the dance, but also bringing live jazz music to the community.

Bullies Ballerinas Jazz Dance Company it became.

ACT 2 — THE REHEARSAL — SCENE 13

The Hey Days

1990 — 2000 were my sugar sweet years.

Having come through the grief enough to 'live' again, it was so uplifting to have the remedy of dance as my medicine. Bullies Ballerinas provided a complete renewal and opened me to a 'birthing mentality'.

I was either giving birth to a new production, project or baby!

After years of wondering at what point as a dancer, I could take time out to start a family, here was the perfect opportunity. As founder and artistic director of Bullies, I could make that choice, and the youngest company member, Liam Moses, (26 hours of labour!!!) was soon born.

I can see me now, heavily pregnant, watching the company perform at The Sadlers Wells Lilian Bayliss Theatre — *Jazz Umbrella* from the Charleston of the 1920s to Hip Hop of the 90s a journey through the history of jazz dance.

Magnificent!

"Can You MC Our Summer Programme?"

Now that was a 'drop the mic' moment, a call worth waiting for.

We had performed our production *Barefeet and Crazy Legs* at The Purcell Rooms, Southbank, to a standing ovation.

"*Barefeet and Crazy Legs, a conversation between traditional African and Jazz dance, forging a dazzling fusion of traditional forms with a decidedly British buzz…Daring and inventive yet grounded in history and tradition, this work presents jazz dance as a living, breathing entity!*"

Our publicity was **spot on**.

Jeanefer and I created a foot stomping, high energy, live African and Jazz music, audience participation, sell-out production that left the audience wanting for more. I recall it being difficult to clear the auditorium every single night!

And now here was 'that' call.

"You mean MC as in Master of Ceremony?"

"Yes, we'd like the 'Pearl and Jean show' to host our six-week summer programme at The Royal Festival Hall? Are you up for it?"

"Of course!"

Jean and I had never MC'd an event. yes, we knew how to engage with an audience and get people dancing but MC officially…? Well, there was only one way to find out.

"I've got nothing to wear" I said to Jean. I was now pregnant with baby number two and SO bloated and uncomfortable. But the show must go on… and what a **show** we produced!

Michael, baby number two was born months later… three hours of labour. That's more like it!

And the calls kept on coming…

The British Council invited us as a multi-cultural company to represent Britain abroad. There were European dates, but the highlight was the Southern and South Africa tour.

1994 saw the end to Apartheid rule and Nelson Mandela was sworn in as the first Black President of South Africa. Six years later there we were, Bullies Ballerinas invited to work with mixed race/diverse groups bridging the gap between 'colour' and class.

Now that's a **valued privilege**!

We experienced racism and we were embraced. We asserted our authority over 'white supremacy' — evidently a first for some. We choreographed on the most talented individuals, our workshops full of African rhythmic vibrancy, and we revamped our production *Jazz Umbrella* especially for CHOGM — The Commonwealth Heads of Government Meeting hosted in Durban South Africa. What an honour!

***

Over the next 10 years Bullies toured three productions; *Jazz Umbrella*, *Rhythm Circus* and *Barefeet and Crazy Legs*, adapting the programme to accommodate a variety of performance venues, small to large scale theatre, art centres, festivals, and social events.

The company consisted of a pool of amazing dancers and musicians that we pulled on as per the performance or teacher requirements.

Some dancers lacked teaching experience, so we trained them using the Bullies ethos and style: *"The session is never about you, but always about the individuals in the room. How much can you tune in and adapt to suit their needs? Your need is to bring them such a feel-good experience that they are eager to thrive."*

More often than not when holding auditions, many of the dancers lacked jazz dance grit, so again we would have to train them, get them rooted in the authenticity of styles.

The challenges of funding were a constant worry and as for budgeting...

I developed a migraine every time.

I was juggling the two boys with tours and rehearsals and thank goodness for having a great partner in Tom, who covered my absences.

But I started to feel the pangs of always handing the boys over to childminders and others, and it started to niggle.

I loved my work. Loved awakening the creativity of others and loved the confidence boosting injection of the Bullies' style.

We really did make jazz dance accessible for all. Oh, the joy of ninety plus people of all ages and backgrounds dancing together, beaming and unified through dance. It took my breath away every time.

As for women groups… to watch individuals shift from hiding in a corner to boldly strutting across the floor… **magic!**

And the many stroppy 'I don't want to be here' teenagers who had not chosen to dance; we would weave them in, gently encouraging them to participate as DJ and then to offer constructive ideas to the group based on their observation… inclusivity always being key… wonderment!

Dancers and non-dancers alike, achieved great things and surprised themselves every time. Even the challenging moments soon dissolved into more creative outlets.

The empowerment spell of Bullies Ballerinas and the healing power of dance proved to be a great mix. But all good things come to an end.

***

After 10 years of touring nationally and internationally the juggle of motherhood and the running of the company began to take its toll.

Jeanefer and I were having talks about creating the first ever London Jazz Dance Festival. We were being directed to the Mayor of London's office for further discussion.

You'd expect me to be jumping for joy. But I was **exhausted** and in **overwhelm**.

We were highly respected. We had flipped the perception of 'jazz dance being a clown amongst the arts', but there was something greater in the air.

We, the *Pearl and Jean Show*, had reached a ceiling of complexity and it was scary.

After a decade of pumping our artistic souls into the company, we felt we had nothing more to offer each other.

Had we been in that position today, we'd have found a business or a life coach to help bring clarity about what and how next. We would have found a 'Pearl'.

But we had no sense of such an option, and it was a different time. There were no coaches available to us, indeed we wouldn't have known what that was anyway.

It still amazes me how we managed to run a successful company for 10 years with very little business acumen. Along the way we had accessed admin support, thank goodness, but clearly we needed more than that.

We sent out feelers to connect with those who might be able to guide us, but finally we settled on time out and took a one-year sabbatical.

I loved being at home and spending quality, uninterrupted time with the boys. It was so good to know there was no tour or reason to leave home.

At the end of the year, I made the hardest decision but the right decision, and that was to move on from the company — a 'Pearlicious moment' you could say — time to go our separate ways.

The jazz dance company so desired at one time, had reached the end of its cycle of life.

The 10 years with Bullies Ballerinas was phenomenal. The gift of dancing with my best friend, AND still remaining best friends, was celebratory.

But it was time to call it 'a wrap'; to let go.

Bullies Ballerinas Jazz Dance Productions, as it was now known, was the Pearl and Jean show. One without the other would not be the same and the thought of continuing without me in the picture didn't make sense. It was the dynamic duo or nothing.

Jeanefer was placed in a premature position of having to agree to it being the end. But if life has taught me one thing, it's that every 'death' produces a rebirth.

Jeanefer, now Jeanefer Jean–Charles MBE, is a renowned Creative Director and Mass Movement Choreographer recognised for her record-breaking achievements and contribution to dance. Woo hoo!

One door closes, another one opens.

Reasons, Seasons and Lifetimes (RSL)

People come into your life for a **Reason**, **Season**, or **Lifetime**.

I am pleased to say the Pearl and Jean story didn't end there. Our friendship has stood the wealth of time and together we continue to work and support each other both in life and throughout our creative and new endeavours.

Many of team Bullies are still in contact, and three members in particular, Martha, Leon and Vik, I haven't been able to get rid of. (Love you really!)

We remain close friends and are forever in each other's corner, providing support, advice and inspiration for creative projects. We co-create and are even known to tread the boards together every now and then. And as for our legendary 'come dine with me' gatherings, complete with an array of puddings and cake, no reunion would be the same without it!

We came together for a reason.

In Bullies we found our season.

We are blessed with the friendship of a lifetime.

SYMPHONY

*If life were a Symphony
what instrument would you be?*

*Do you belong to the brass section, the strings, woodwind,
or perhaps you are more percussive in style?
What would you bring to the melody?*

*Can you imagine a conductor trying to guide
a double bass player who believes it to be an oboe?
What a disaster that would be!*

*If life was a Symphony of four movements
with differing tempos
fast, slow and others in between
What would be your movement
1,2,3, or 4?
Slowly does it, as you explore.*

*If life were a Symphony of pure music to be made
and your instrument was as clear as day,
imagine a flute with which to serenade,
creating magical compositions of truth, to aid.*

What would be your contribution,
your tune?
Gifts of sound to set the stage,
propelling life forwards with orchestral grace.

If life were a Symphony
yours to be made
co-creating and making music in every way
with your speciality of high grade
how would you conduct yourself?
How would you play?

ACT 2 — THE REHEARSAL — SCENE 14

Heartbeat of Homeopathy

"That's disgusting!" screamed 5-year-old Liam.

It was disgusting, but my intentions were positive and it was for his own good!

"You drink this tea, and you can have a big handful of milk chocolate buttons," I bribed.

Liam had been diagnosed with potential asthma. The thought of a life on inhalers didn't work for me, then a friend suggested Chinese Medicine. But it was a big ask of a child.

The brewed herbs really did taste and smell disgusting. I had to find another way. I was introduced to Homeopathy, complementary medicine. It worked like magic. I had to find out more.

I attended an introduction to Homeopathy open day.

Oh, oh, **warning bells**... I tingled throughout... There was something going on here, I knew it well... and within a crazy heartbeat, I insisted on an interview that day!

I was told I would have to apply at a later date, but I knew that tingle, there was no "no" for an answer. Yes, I made that clear.

I received my interview and returned home with a four-year Homeopathy Course on the horizon. I was to become a Homeopath, a Practitioner of Alternative Medicine!

I loved those four years; fascinating insights and learning, beautiful inquisitive people, lunches, walks in Regent's Park, the early misty morning heron greeting ... It was super intense and challenged me in endless ways.

I had to learn the complete picture of individual remedies, and there are hundreds!

Anatomy and Physiology was fascinating and caused brain strain, but it was worth it!

Who would have thought?

Here I was on a new path, in the bliss of another 'new dance'.

***

I qualified in 2006 with a 'Licentiate of Homeopathy' tightly under my belt.

The psychology and therapy of Homeopathy, in particular due to 'My Body Is My Temple' episode of Scene 13, sparked passionate enquiry.

AND — and this is an incredible and — I couldn't help myself relating all things mind-body-spirit to the world of dance!!!

There was new awakening…

If a dancer knew of the mind-body connection, how thoughts and feelings impact your body, that would certainly change the negative self-talk, wouldn't it…?

If leaders in dance had this insight, surely this would encourage a more positive and empowering training and performance culture.

There would be fewer mental health issues and injuries that's for sure.

There was something in this…

I could feel a buzz…

I was 'dancing from the gut' in truth, once more.

"Before you leave. What kind of Homeopath will you be?" Asked the tutor.

"The one you trained us to be these past four years" I silently replied with sarcasm.

"Now you have the knowledge," he continued, "your task is to go out there and to find out who you are as a Homeopath."

What the...??

That just didn't make any sense!

And yet of course it made absolute sense.

***

The first few years I did my best to practise 'pure' homeopathy with a private practice in various wellbeing centres offering one-to-one consultations; but the magnetic pull of dance continued.

I started to speak publicly on the mind-body connection, held a successful event titled "Body Wise — A mind-body approach to a healthier dancer" at The Royal Society of Medicine. Big up to the national body for dance, One Dance UK, for having the courage to support me at a time when there was no such thinking or belief systems!

I was shunned by an audience of doctors, surgeons and conventional practitioners at a performance arts medicine event. They were so bored, disinterested and dismissive of my 'hocus pocus'. "Mind and body connected? PAH!!!!"

I held health and wellbeing talks and workshops with dance students at my old training college Weekend Arts College (WAC).

And for several years explored movement as an empowerment tool at Swindon Dance, Centre for Advanced Training.

There was however still something missing...

What do I call it, this health, wellbeing, dance and performance empowerment thing...?

I had definitely created a new blend of passions — must be my style — first with Bullies and now here with 'this', whatever this is...

If I could call it a methodology or a technique, if I could name it... that would be a mighty fine thing...

I spoke with my dear friend, Irish dancer Máire Clerkin. We talked of Bullies and how I seemed to be replicating my excellence.

And then she added one more feature to the mix.

"You've always healed through dance."

I have...?

ACT 2   THE REHEARSAL   SCENE 15

Divine Download

I am sitting in silence.

No music accompanying my meditation.

I am searching for answers.

My workshops produce profound results.

Deep change appears for participants.

Often, they shed tears.

Transformational dance...?

I have now also entered the professional speaking world.

I am President of The Professional Speaking Association, London Region, and I dare to allow movement to lead the way.

I dance when I speak.

I get the audience singing, beating rhythms, playing.

But I bring a censored version of 'Pearl' to the stage because I am still uncertain of my mix.

*"Live with the questions
whilst the heart dances with the answers."*

- Malidoma Patrice Somé
Of Water and Spirit

And then through the silence of meditation, I hear...

Pearl, are you in tune or out of tune?

Whose dance are you dancing to?

Why so off beat?

I couldn't **believe it.**

A voice was using vocabulary of dance as if everyday language.

It was on a roll. I dared not move in case it stopped.

I sat still holding my breath too afraid to exhale.

Enough of the crazy legs!

Ball-change and ground in stillness

Transfer your weight in faith.

It now flowing at the fastest 5,6,7,8.

A full chorus line of movement, health, wellbeing, the lot, ready to give any Strictly Come Dancing routine a run for its 10, 10, 10!

Here was my renewal, the **vocabulary of dance**, as if a hidden language now flowing free, to motivate myself and for others to see.

When I folded Bullies and found Homeopathy, I truly believed I had hung up my dance shoes for good. Little did I know the universe had new and exciting plans for this 'soul food'.

"When the student is ready
The teacher will appear
When the question is asked
Then the answer is heard
When we are truly ready to receive
Then what we need
Will become available"

- John Gray

Author

ACT 2   THE REHEARSAL   SCENE 16

Angel

"Why don't you call your work the rhythmic remedy or something like that?"

I'm in a café. It's a networking event. I'm with a complete stranger; the angel I had never met before and have yet to meet ever since.

"You constantly speak of rhythms and cycles of life, rhythms within nature, rhythms of the body, never mind your jazz dance and the remedy of Homeopathy… why not call your method… rhythmic remedy or something like that?"

What did he just say?!

Immediately I thought of an expression I often use — "the answer sits at the end of your nose; you just have to see it."

The irony. Here I was with the answer dangling at the end of my nose.

And I couldn't see.

He did.

Whoever you are

Wherever you are

I am so grateful for you

You helped me see

At the end of my nose

The mystery.

The Rhythmic Remedy®

A Movement inspired

Holistic approach

To Personal and Professional Growth

Or...

The Rhythmic Remedy®

Transformational Dance

Or...

The Rhythmic Remedy®

Where Dance meets Personal Growth

Yippee

Playtime!

KNOWING WHAT YOU KNOW

*You only know what you know
When you know it
Until such time
You only know what you know
But once you know
Once you have the gift of knowing
Then and only then can you do something about it
Then you have choice
Then you have insight for change
Until you are awake
You are asleep
Sleepwalking
But once awake...*

*Here comes the sun, doo-doo-doo-doo
Here comes the sun, and I say,
It's alright*

*Nine times out of ten
The soul-ution sits at the end of your nose*

Did you know...?

VIBRANT AND VULNERABLE

I am vibrant and vulnerable
Fabulous and flawed
And I own it!

I let go of the ideals
The made-up stories
The should have's
The expectations that lead you down the paths of disappointment
I drop it, release the weight and the trappings of it all!

The pressure of perfectionism
I leave at the convenience store
I am taking the imperfection ride
For the lie of perfectionism
I see you
you false guide.

I am vibrant and vulnerable
Fabulous and flawed
Sometimes on point
Sometimes splat on the floor
But never floored!
No matter the wake-up call.

There was so much flowing
So many reasons to pause, reflect, dissect
Her healing steps
Each one providing
A deep, deep stretch

She felt free to take a pause
To stretch at this time

Gift of the rehearsal
It is yours to unwind
Return refreshed
Alert to new thoughts
The next epiphany
Is on the dance floor

ACT 2   THE REHEARSAL   SCENE 17

Hey Mr DJ

Have you ever been on a dance floor getting into the groove, boogieing to your heart's content, feeling at one with all, smiling unified in the beat?

And then the DJ shifts into another gear and suddenly what once felt so good now feels completely out of place.

You struggle to find your rhythm, you have two left feet. What was in sync with others, is gone... being in tune with yourself... gone!

And so, what to do?

You can blame the DJ for messing with the tunes whilst strutting off the dance floor or you can adapt and shuffle to a new groove.

Which is it to be?

***

Revisiting past scenes reminded me of how external circumstances can hold you steady or flip you in a matter of seconds.

How the DJ of life if not personally approved, can send you in a spin, have you 'rewind' or dance to the tune of others at a whim.

Finding your groove, not an easy move, a minor scratch can have you pop, crackle, lean back.

You may skip a beat, jump from foot to foot, due to a 'record burn' but no step is too hot, when 'feeling hot, hot, hot', and dancing to the *rhythm of your soul*.

Finding your groove, such an easy move... right...??

ACT 2 — THE REHEARSAL — SCENE 18

A Dance Battle

I developed two internal opponents, a dance off between victim and victorious.

Victim wished to stamp her feet on a bed of nails and remain in the zone of the painful past.

Victorious on the other hand, chose to tip toe through the tulips... no matter what.

They were always at battle, pulling here and pulling there, a tug of war of proverbial dance moves, each determined as the other, creating a stance worthy of any street dance challenge.

Ladies and gentlemen... on your right we have victim, the old groove stuck on repeat! To my left, victorious with pure happy feet! Which is it to be...?

DJ... Hit it!

"Everybody was Kung fu Fighting (huh!)

Those cats were fast as lightning (Ha!)

In fact it was a little bit frightening

But they fought with expert timing."

Hold up, wait a minute... DJ spin another tune.

"I can see clearly now the rain is gone
 I can see all obstacles in my way
 gone are the dark clouds that had me blind
It's gonna be a bright (bright)
Bright (bright) sunshiny day."

So, victim, stop pretending you are still waiting for a storm to pass.

Start singing and dancing in the rain with victorious, barefoot in the grass!

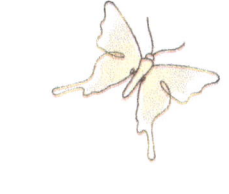

Feeling Great

I once worked on a production called *Feeling Great...no matter what.* No matter what, you hold onto your feel good. No matter what, you keep a tight grip on your happiness, your peace of mind. No matter who, no matter the hurts, the traumas, no matter the past, yours is to remember it is just that, **the past** — done, dusted, finished.

As my friend Lucinda sings...

"Pack up your weakness,

consider your goodness,

let the past be the past

and let this moment be true."

The past, so easy to stay locked in the past and miss the **present** gift of today.

Have you noticed how easy it is to have one foot in the past and one foot in the future?

That is one heck of a split!

And how about this as a food for thought: *past memories are false anyway*, so coloured do they become over the years, in that Chinese whispers' way.

The question is, how true is true…?

I am retelling my story as I see it today, but if I were to be whizzed back to that moment in time, I'm sure there would be an element of … oh, is **that** the truth, the whole truth and nothing but the truth?

Remaining stuck in the past and focussing on the future is a convenient way of avoiding that which needs attention now, that's my take on it anyway.

*Perhaps I do not wish to really '**see**'…?*

*Perhaps I do not wish to **take responsibility**?*

*Perhaps I actually feel more comfortable in the **space of the shadows**?*

*Perhaps I am **attached to the struggle**…yuk!*

In the past my wings were certainly clipped, I have the stories to prove it, and yes, there was a ripple effect, but how long did I keep myself grounded?

How long did it take for me to dare flap my wings (Phoenix rise) and take off… no matter what?

> *"Examining the past can help clarify many of our problems, but healing doesn't occur in the past — it occurs in the present."*
>
> \- Marianne Williamson

Certainly, revisiting the past is an important step but watch for the indulgence it can bring, which is what I've had to remind myself of again and again.

Let it go... Let it be, let it be, oh let it be!

Place your focus not on your past-self, but who you have **become** and who you **becoming** in a natural, unpressured way. Trust in your process. Keep the faith!

MOMENT OF STILLNESS

Sitting still

I take a few deep, slow breaths

To calm the speed of my mind,

To drop into the loving presence within my heart.

I continue until the silence is ready to provide

I let the past be the past

And this moment be true

The choice is mine

As it is for you

Feeling Great, no matter what

You choose...

ACT 2   THE REHEARSAL   SCENE 20

P.E.A.R.L

On a bus journey, one evening, I find my mind doodling, drifting into space, the space that led you into trouble as a child at school, for not paying enough attention.

That wonderful, creatively, magical, Aladdin's carpet space of make believe.

I hear myself ask, what if the name 'Pearl' was an acronym?

And within a split second of a whisper, with no mention of abracadabra, I hear:

Positively

Enthusiastic

About

Real

Lives

WOW. Where did that come from?!

I sat giggling; 'something or someone' was having fun.

Hi...

Hi,

I Am P.E.A.R.L,

And I Am **P**ositively **E**nthusiastic **A**bout **R**eal **L**ives

Which means...

I Am positively enthusiastic about YOU;

The Love of you.

A perfect partner

To swing with

To the rhythms of life.

Care to dance?

Let's Jive!

[laughing]

Oh, the joys of **wonder** and **play**.

I missed my stop but that's ok.

It was worth it

To enjoy my heart's meanderings in this way

How often do you doodle on a day to day...?

ACT 2 — THE REHEARSAL — SCENE 21

The Cards Don't Lie

Oh, the cards certainly do not lie.

Many moons ago, I joined an all-black cast of the musical, *Carmen Jones*, at the Old Vic Theatre, London.

Carmen Jones, based on Bizet's opera, *Carmen*, a tragic love story.

Three reasons why I was so thrilled:

Dorothy Dandridge as the sultry Carmen and Harry Belafonte as the handsome Joe. I had watched the 1954 all-black production as a child; a film where black actors played 'real characters' and not a janitor, or maid, or servant of a kind, real people!

If you recall my childhood Swanee story, of sitting cross legged with my nose inches away from the TV screen, watching the song and dance of the black and white minstrel show...? Then you will appreciate the awe of *Carmen Jones*.

Second excitement...

I had received a call to audition. Not the usual open cattle market dancer try out, but a private *Carmen Jones* invitation, where they knew my name and welcomed me with such warmth and respect. I had arrived!

And now here I was at the prestigious Old Vic, dancing my dance with an all-black cast of British and American artists. Me, little Pearl, transported through the screen, manifested. *Beat out dat Rhythm on a Drum!*

And so why 'the cards don't lie?

There is a dramatic scene in the musical when Carmen is having her tarot cards read and the prediction is grim. She is having none of it, objecting to all of it, and the three fortune tellers sing repeatedly, 'the cards don't lie'.

And you know what...

The cards don't lie.

Over the years as part of my every day personal growth and wellbeing practise, I use Oracle cards — a divination tool, that encourages and enhances your intuition.

The drawing of each card brings a mind-blowing, on point message and the transformative power of the cards, the divine guidance received. It's like... magic!

The cards don't lie.

1. I draw a card from my oracle deck, Hindu Goddess, KALI, a celestial being associated with death and rebirth. The card reads "Endings and Beginnings". I shudder and shake uncontrollably as I meditate; have a major embodied experience. This is not an everyday occurrence... but with grace I acknowledge her 'presence'.

2. I'm attending a workshop. I walk past a bookshelf, a book falls at my feet, KALI. What is going on? Do I buy it? No. I place it back on the shelf. The workshop facilitator mentions Kali within a second of me thinking the name. Note: this is not a Goddess workshop but a light worker workshop. I had felt the pull to explore what this 'lightworker' thing was about. If it was about spreading love, light and positive energy into the world, then yep, why not check it out.

3. During the rehearsal period of my life, reflecting and exploring the many scenes and stories, no matter how often I shuffled the cards, yep, you may have guessed it... Goddess KALI; "Endings and Beginnings' — The old must be released so that the new can enter."

Clearly there was a plan. I took note.

***

For a whole year, on a regular basis she, powerful Hindu Goddess KALI, my guiding light, would be there, forever close, reminding me to trust the process and embrace the change of endings and beginnings. No matter what showed up, the life, death, life cycles that appeared, remain unshakeable, carefree, in preparation for the curves of life ahead of me.

***

The cards don't lie.

FOOD FOR THOUGHT...

"What must I give more death to today, in order to generate more life?

What do I know should die, but am hesitant to do so?

What must die in me in order for me to love?

What not-beauty do I fear?

Of what use is the power of the not beautiful to me today?

What should die today?

What should live?

What life am I afraid to give birth to?

If not now, when? "

- Clarissa Pinkola Estés

Women Who Run With The Wolves

EMPTY ROOM

My head is pounding.
The zig zagged migraine aura is swimming across my eyes,
A shimmering light, encouraging I shut them tight.
I don't.

My teeth are sore,
I have clearly been grinding.
I am tense.
I ask for recompense;
Denied.
I have come to an end,
An empty room awaits

Ghostly visitors of the past, now removed,
Touched by a profound sense of their presence
But free to make new.

Enter the empty room
Internal antennae guiding every move,
No looking back.
The past will keep you trapped,
Freedom is in forward motion.

Flex and flow,
Fast and slow,
With a fullness of life
Only you can ignite

Black Pearl
Precious little girl,
Who knows what the years will bring
Break a leg

Good luck!

Your empty room is gesturing you in.

WHAT NEXT...?

With all this behind me
and 'of' me,
what next?
who next?
how...?

Scenes jammed in the projection of my mind
I wonder what it is I wish for here and now

I know it will come...

"Life is a dance between making it
happen and letting it happen."
- Arianna Huffington

Act III

IN THE WINGS

[*overture*]

I'm coming home
I'm coming home to where I'm meant to be
Where no one tells me who I'm supposed to be
Where I can go dancing in the rain
Close my eyes
It's blissful to say

I'm coming home
What will be will be
It's taken some time
For me to be me
I look in the mirror and I know what's going on
It's so much clearer
Nothing feels wrong
'Cause I'm coming home

I'm coming home to the place inside
That I've shut out all my life
Where I can run wild and free
My eyes open, it's blissful to see

I'm coming home...

- Jenny Plant

[Voiceover]

Ring the bells that still can ring
Forget your perfect offering
There is a crack, a crack in everything
That's how the light gets in

Anthem
- Leonard Cohen

ACT 3　　　　　　　　IN THE WINGS　　　　　　　　SCENE 1

Heartbeats

Imagine standing in the wings of life, the area out of sight, where you come and go, a space where you and only you silently 'know'...

Imagine you stepping out into the bright light, every step witnessed. How do you feel?

Can you imagine...

[heartbeats]

Your heartbeat at an unhealthy rate, anticipatory anxiety at its height, a mix of 'bring it on' ready to rock, juxtaposed with pure stage fright.

A dark void awaits... you may even pass out.

[heartbeats]

Can you?
Will you?
Do you have **what it takes...**?

It is **now** or **never**.
You can't afford to make a mistake.
And there it is, old skool training, mistake, mistake, **mistake!**

But hang on, haven't you done the work, to be stood here in the 'wings'?

Prepped front, back, in-out, outside in?

Do you think you would make it here, if you hadn't acknowledged your worth...?

Settle down

Stop being a clown.

Less of the wild imaginings,

You have nothing to prove

Other than to yourself

Stop with the outside looking in.

Get back to trust,

Release the pressure,

Allow the pleasure in.

Simply bring your best.

See, believe in your success.

My mantra advice to you

It's a temporary spot,

Pivotal too

One step, two step,

Aww, look at you...

Stepping

[heartbeats]

Into a New Groove

Finding Your Groove

If you recall, way back in ACT II Scene 9, 'Permission to go Solo' I stood in the wings shaking. I allowed anxiety to mess with my performance. My response was to dance as if I had been set a solo, and eventually the gift of that time became apparent... one of self-trust.

This turning point has served both me and others over the years. And then came this icing on the cake...

"I walk onto the stage and sometimes speak to more than a thousand people at a time. I can't imagine dealing with the pressure of having to convince myself that I have something special to offer. I don't try to. I don't have to impress anyone, and if I am not thinking I have to, there's nothing to do but relax. I walk out on stage without feeling the need to make people think I'm special, because I know I am not. I just talk to friends, casually and with enthusiasm. That's it. There isn't anything else. Everything else is an illusion..."

Marianne Williamson

How brilliant is that? Talk about keeping things real. And what an analogy for life!

When I first read this paragraph, it just blew my mind, stopped me in my tracks... I don't have to impress anyone therefore I have nothing to prove. Light bulb!

FREEDOM!

All those years I'd been so concerned about how I perform and wanting to impress others and receive approval. All those years so outside looking in, not inside-looking out, as if I didn't count. All that **anxiety**... that paragraph really brought things home.

I, no more special than you; you, no more special than me, no special-dom kingdom required.

All of us, every individual on an even keel, no superiority levels, no power games, goodness me, there is so much freedom in that!

Be it an interview, audition, a presentation, a difficult conversation to be had... No matter the role or situation, no more special than each other. Join me: **"no more special than each other."** How liberating is that!

This was **HUGE** and had me *gaze afar* into a scale of possibilities and even the subject of 'sales'.

Sales

All this 'special-dom' anxiety was based on a subtle form of sales. Selling myself in the hope of the next gig, selling myself in the hope of praise, approval and so on.

Here was the pressure...

FOR SALE: A product not fully authentic, wrapped in all kinds of packaging and unwelcome voices, stepping to the tune of others.

Isn't it any wonder I experienced so much angst, self-doubt and such...?

Can you relate to this? You must be able to relate to this, moments in your life when you have been too busy 'selling yourself' and not grounded in your groove; that clear confident sense of who you are and the best you can provide.

That's why people speak of sales versus service. Where is your focus, the former or the latter...?

The answer to that question sits within your 'heartbeat'.

This was a new step to **finding my groove**.

"What is it that makes you so comfortable on stage?"

"You appear so at ease."

"How is it you can do that?"

Different people at different times all with the same questions, as I rocked to my groove.

The proof was in the pudding. Yum! Pure delight.

"You bring so much joy when you present."

"I cried in awe as I watched you dance."

"What's your secret ingredient?"

I had narrowed it down to those three words

N_ T _ _ _ G

T_

P_ _ V _

All I can be, is all I can be, in any given moment.

I am not looking for the number of 'likes' but hope you like what you see.

I surrender and trust all is designed as it is meant to be.

I have

nothing

to

prove

But to stand in the wings with my beauty, wisdom, knowledge, vulnerability, uncertainty, humility, courage...

All of it

No one to impress but me

                              I

                            have

                           nothing

                             to

                            prove.

PEACE

"The Song of Life has a beautiful rhythm.
At times we forget the lyrics,
but as long as good people like you provide the melody,
life's music plays on."

- Unknown Author

GIFT FOR THE SOUL

Life is unfolding exactly as it is meant to.
To resist the lessons causes pain and stress
Therefore, I choose to accept everything as it is.
I accept myself, others and the world.
Acceptance is an expression of love
That leads to peace
And becomes a powerful catalyst for change.

- Raja Yoga Meditation

Acceptance

I have thrown many a hissy fit over the years, pointed the finger and blamed.

Nothing dissipates such self-indulgence like the **Art of Acceptance**.

Acceptance is like sprinkling stardust on adverse situations and watching it magically transform.

Today, when victim attempts to point the finger in anger, judgement and frustration, I sprinkle the stardust of acceptance.

What does this do?

It shows the thumb pointing right back at you, plus three fingers too.

[Try it. Point your index finger and see...]

...This is how it was

this is how it hurt

this is how I chose to respond

to believe

make it mine

even though it weren't.

I can accept that people behave badly

I behave badly too

accept I may have been a trigger

it takes two

I accept I may never receive an apology

come to know the reasons why

apology at some point becomes neither here nor there

I accept the healing is mine to decide.

I forgive

at least

work on the premise of forgiveness

for what you do for others

you do for you

And so...

I accept my innocence

I wear the other shoe

accept the innocence of others

allowing compassion and empathy

to shine through

*There is **freedom** in acceptance*

incredibly liberating if you choose

to accept the story of your life

what more could you ask of you?

To dance with peace in your heart

to be of a lighter mood

surely it's worth looking at the fingers

pointing right back at you.

A BRIDGE...

Do I sound like a prophet?
A leading light?
A spiritual guide who is gentle and kind?
Not wishing to spoil things,
have to admit,
not in a million years
could I have anticipated
what came next.

With all the enlightenment
spiritual insights
and pride of my wisdom years,
could I be the opposite;
a different type of blood gushing
pumping through my veins.

That I could be a furious woman
raging at our cruel world
Pointing the finger relentlessly
without any concern

One finger one thumb keeps moving

[agitated]

One finger one thumb keeps moving
One finger one thumb keeps moving
We'll all be merry and bright

I could sweep it under the carpet so I can be nice

But...

There had been too many injustices

Too many times

Too many bad things

Done to me and mine

Propelling me and past wounds towards a mighty front line

And so, to...

BLACK

BLACK

It had been building and growing in strength over previous months. So much anger, irritation welling up inside, I knew it couldn't simply be mine.

No. Seriously. After all the healing I had been through, it definitely wasn't mine.

Sitting in meditation, I envisioned a wishing well, a well full of broken bones, thoughts, hopes, wants, desires, and dreams, frozen in time.

So much pain, emotional strain with the sickliest feeling in my gut, a growing nausea of fear, I felt I might throw up.

I kept on thinking, "This isn't me, this isn't who I am… This is beyond me, it must be… I feel so overwhelmingly wretched."

And then as if to break the power of the meditative spell, I heard the word 'BLACK'.

Oh…? And again 'BLACK'.

I instinctively grabbed pen and paper. There was so much energy.

BLACK… BLACK… **BLACK!**

This was not my imagination, my deep instinct assured me. This '**it**' was a call from those who came before me...

BLACK

A colour dense, heavy, intensity.

BLACK

A life of oppression, less than, lacking.

BLACK

A secondary, after thought, last, last, always last.

BLACK

History perverted, no history, blank, domination, broken, psyche mangled, taut manipulation, racial programming, chipped with fear, on a robotic production line.

BLACK

Struggles, subservience glorified, servant to this, servant to that, pinny-apron attached.

BLACK

Make good. Make nice. Smile in that "Swanee, how I love you, how I love you..."

Cut the click!
Enough of this
Even — bought into — this, click!

Anger, irritation, past hurts, presently, presenting.
I've been broken,
Watched my race broken
Lived my race crushed into smithereens, scattered and displaced.
Moving away more than towards,
we hang by the throat
a necklace of exasperating hope.

BLACK

Let's turn this around my **beautiful Ancestry**.
I hear your cries
I feel your pain,
the pound of your heartbeat as if entertained.

Not.

And yet a deep lingering scent of your **RISE**.
What a surprise

BLACK

Bold black
Strength
Full of passion, purpose, power
unbroken spirits calling, demanding, releasing, the rebirth of...

BLACK

For you,
For me,
For humanity,
Radical forgiveness and liberation is key.
Surgically removing all blame, shame and negativity,
scrubbing away the fatigue of eternity,
setting my battered soul free

BLACK

Incubated no more,
       chained no more
              shackled less more
                      weightlessness yearning for

FREEDOM

Free in mind, body, and soul

FREEDOM

For you
For me
For my Ancestry
Flying Free...
One more thing of clarity...
For you too may have been the oppressor

What?!!

Past life uncertainty

Today in a black body
but who knows previously...?
My heart stops, stunned
Karmic philosophy
and so, forgiveness, radical forgiveness is key.

For you
For me
For humanity

BLACK

Oh, my Ancestry...
A cry to remain unshackled and broken-free,
To light a lamp of kindness, that induces liberty
Kindness, let that be the flame that melts the hearts of pain and evil's gain.
Be reborn
full of hope
with dreams and emotional exclaim

BLACK

No to being crushed.
No to this whitewashed plain.

But let kindness be the root of all humanity,

let that be the **start of a new game**.

This is a call to action as never before

no more hopelessly looking out to shore.

This simmering anger and strong urge to lash out,

keeping you stuck in the ugliness of man's claws,

know that this is the perfect spell of traps,

So, kick open 'dem' doors!

Warning… The 'face of self-violence' is at the fore.

Kindness

collective kindness,

we implore you for this restart.

In the spirit world we fly free,

with reclaimed self-love,
polished up nicely

But your world of continued density and disharmony,

ignoring history

is like a magnetic force, dancing with our peace, our light, pulling us to a continual dark genealogy.

Yours, is to melt away,

to let go, to set free,

to fire up freedom and truly be,

to feed and nourish an unbound mentality,

reawaken healthy bones of one's ancestry.

Kindness,

please collective kindness,

we implore you for this restart,

have us dance on this plain,

a merry tap dance.

BLACK

W**iped out** and stunned by this surreal experience, I dropped my pen, whilst gulping and taking several deep breaths.

"What was the significance of this?" I wondered, "Indeed, what was this?!"

Left brain logic began to kick in, but I was wise enough to know that in this space, right brain intuition must lead and soon I started to note its personal significance.

Safe — Space — Honesty...

Since May 2020 and the Black Lives Matter Movement, I had been developing growing agitations. The more I saw black people and people of colour in lead roles within the public domain, the more I found myself in a bittersweet reflection.

Yes, it was great that we of the global majority, were at last being given openings within media, advertising, leadership roles and more.

But at the same time, glaringly obvious was the conscious decision of the decision makers, the powers that be, to suppress us, to keep us small, wings clipped and lacking in opportunity, poisoning my people's genealogy.

If it wasn't for the brutal death of George Floyd and the collective unified 'white-black' global outrage, where might we be...?

They taketh away
They giveth now
Might they choose to remove, when we are not looking out
And we remain forever puppets on a string...?!
The seed of this 'visit' was mine.
I was whipping up a storm
feeling thunderous with life,
my woes of the present,
inflaming past ghostly cries.

Message understood and received.

Kindness, forgiveness, compassion indeed.

A return to the fullness of love being key,

for the complete liberation and unity of 'WE'.

How could I not see?

Perhaps due to the immersion of the struggle of collective energy,
my thoughts, feelings, and empathy,
now with an invitation for renewed vitality

Stop this peaceless heart closing charade
open and expand out wide wings of gratitude,
your ancestors coming to your aid.

BLACK

I breathe in for count one and breathe out for count one.

Breathe in for two and out for two and so on, until such time I let go, and flow with my natural inhale, exhale rhythm.

BLACK

How was it I could have such a profound experience and receive communication in this way?

Those who came before me, of the spirit world, coming to my aid?

They could see I was about to 'exit the stage' due to rising, limiting, negative energy outrage.

My ancestors coming to my aid as clear as day.

Wot to say...?

Sixth Sense

I had been experiencing unusual happenings:

- Phone vibration sensations in my pockets, but with no phone present...
- Shake, rattle and roll moments during meditation...
- Gifts of white feathers, a powerful Divine Pendant, Angel coins galore...
- Dreams that produced messages through numbers, songs, even a spot on bioflavonoid supplement for my wellbeing!
- Three Robins, one by one, perched on a Kew Garden bench where I sat in the Mediterranean Garden, each looking me straight in the eye and 'telling me off' I tell you no lie!!
- A Vesica Piscis, two overlapping circles, considered the original symbol of creativity, appeared on my white t-shirt. They matched the vesica piscis emerald pendant I had recently bought. I could not believe it and for a long time refused to wash the t-shirt!
- And of course, there was the message from my mother...

Something was happening and it often unnerved me.

I then met 'K' at a networking event. He happened to mention psychic experiences, as you do, out of the blue... not.

Inside I lit up intrigued. Could **this** be my experience too...?

Dare I share my stories...?

Eventually I summed up the courage. And his no-nonsense response threw me off balance.

"I'd advise you to consider such experiences not as unnatural or supernatural, but **natural** in every way. No 'wow' about things, simply take it in your stride."

"Natural? Did he just say, natural...?" Buzzed a voice in my head.

"After years of being in this space," he continued, "that is really the best advice I can give. Sounds like you are being channelled and opening up to what we all have access to, your psychic awakening."

Psychic awakening?

What me?

Yes you

Couldn't be!

Then it's who?

Roll the camera

Take 1

I'm sitting on a high backed, wooden chair, cocooned in a shawl, I face my altar with its candles, crystals and items of divine love.

My breathing swings deeper and deeper to the calming meditative music, drawing in the silence...

It is 4 a.m.

Divine Hour.

A time celebrated by many cultures and spiritual traditions, recognised for its deep silence and stillness, you could say the calm before the 'storm' of daily life.

A time of solitude, serenity, much mental clarity.

Before the wake of dawn and birds begin to sing.

The image of a male bust flashes through my mind.

I ask, "if you were to have a name what would it be?"

How I knew to ask this question, I still ask of myself today. But my instinct had me surrender to the flow.

"Marius."

I heard, or did I, see...?

The image of a large, winged black, white bird appeared in my mind's eye.

I recognised it but couldn't remember its type.

I grabbed pen and paper and drew the image.

Next stop, web search.

All this happening with instinct as if a normal day occurrence, which it wasn't, but a level of 'known' ease.

Low and behold, there he was, Marius, Roman General, with the symbolism of the Eagle.

Well, I never.

Flabbergasted!

A few weeks later, I visit a garden centre for the first time. I am drawn to the gift shop. What do I see? Posh Marius toiletries. I laugh, then start to hyperventilate and run out of the door!

As the Saint Lucians love to say... "Wot to say...?!"

Take 2

I attend a Goddess workshop. During a visualisation I feel a brush of air pass by as if caressed by a presence. By the end of the session a name traces through my mind. It is an unusual name; Maji. Naturally as soon as I could, I web searched… and yep, Goddess Maji, Goddess of water, fond of pearls! Lol! You couldn't make it up! But more fascinating was the next day, someone contacted me for Homeopathic advice for her mother called… Maji!!

[all together now]

"Wot to say…?!"

Take 3

I wake with two scratches, on the side of both thighs, varying in length, an inch or so. They mirror each other as if I'd undergone an initiation during my sleep.

At first, I was afraid I was petrified, but then I chose to trust that whatever it was, for whatever reason it had taken place, and that I was safe.

And no, it wasn't me having a scratch during the night. It wasn't *just my imagination running away with me*. I literally watched a small cut appear on my thumb just as I shared the story with a friend… confirmation if ever there was one.

The scars left as they came, days later, silently.

I felt the call to write…

I am a powerful soul
I know I am
because of stuff
and I have the scars to prove it.

I am a powerful soul
I know I am
I must be
because of stuff
stuff of this world and out of this world
connecting with me.

I am a powerful soul.
Two cuts on each thigh
should I be concerned
take it in my stride...?

I remain curious...
I must do
for my sanity.

I am a powerful soul.
I know I am
 I must be

Be...

Right! Let's take a closer look at this.

I had my stories.

Had multitude experiences.

I knew what I knew.

I was going to take ownership of the happenings and say YES to whoever, whatever, however, until I came to understand its significance.

I was to give myself 'permission to go solo'

To flow and glide with natural ease

Sixth sense and I dancing a breeze.

There is more to life than the eye can see

It brings with it humility

A speck within the galaxy

How, small, are, we...

I detach, watch, wait and see.

Curious...

And so, to BLACK.

By the time I get to BLACK I am well-seasoned.

I have experienced so many 'supreme natural' variations on a theme that although shocked by the calls' intensity, I am ready, willing and able.

Wot to say...?

But...

Wè, Wè, Wè!

"Where would you have me go
What would you have me do
What would you have me say
And to whom?"

- Marianne Williamson

ACT 3   IN THE WINGS   SCENE 6

A Comedy of Error

Wè, wè, wè

See, see, see

[Kwéyòl]

Wey, wey, wey

[phonetic]

Well, well, well!

[slang]

The universe is having a laugh!

Sa cho, sa cho, sa cho!

Sa show, sa show, sa show!

That's hot, that's hot, that's hot!

Actual Translation…

Oh, my goodness that is so funny, so hilarious, let me catch my breath, if only I could catch my breath!!

Mwen wi tèlman zyé mewn jik pléwé!

I laughed so much I even cried!

Wè, wè, wè!

This has to be one of the funniest days of my life.

I am walking with a friend in the beautiful healing grounds of Kew Gardens. Here we meet to create magic. We have our favourite bench and our grand old tree where we set our 'spells of intention'; this tree holds our accountability.

The lead up had been sixth sense interesting...

I'd left home to catch a train but then felt a pull to return to collect a flyer for my friend and then to return with a second pull to place the flyer in an A5 envelope.

'What's with the envelope?' I thought as I was delayed yet again, but for some reason it appeared important. Who was I to question my intuition.

So, I met my friend, we chatted and then I said I have something for you and handed her the A5 envelope. She responded, and I have something for you, and handed me an identical envelope.

This took me by surprise... what's with the A5 envelopes? We laughed out loud.

"It's not from me," said she.

"Oh, really who is it from?"

"My husband."

I had never met or spoken to her husband.

"I have no idea what he's written, he simply asked me to give this to you."

OK...

And then:

Wè, wè, wè!

Sa cho, Sa cho, Sa cho!

"Dear Pearl,

It was mentioned to me that you are a confident public speaker and that you have very clear political views. I wondered if you'd peruse this manifesto and consider running as *[...Oh, too funny... Wè, wè, wè ...]* as a candidate for Mayor of London!!"

What? Why me?! I haven't a political bone in my body. I am no activist! What did you say to him?!

"It must be because I often mention your views and values on social issues and such."

"Well, wot to say?!" I mimic with the heaviest St. Lucian accent.

Wè, wè, wè!

I am now fanning myself, heat rising.

Two identical A5 envelopes.

A most ridiculous request.

I became intrigued...

I read the manifestos and to my surprise I could relate to it and even had opinions on the points covered. I actually felt aligned with this party, who shall remain nameless. Why nameless? Politics can cause divisions and waste thoughts. The point of sharing this story is bigger than whose politics I am referring to. What I will say: it was not a main party.

Universe!!!!!!

I imagined myself addressing Parliament, giving speeches and being very clear about my reasons for this and reasons for that.

This is so ridiculous, I must meet with this man, if only to thank him for making me lol!

And so I did, on two occasions.

The first meet was to say thanks, but no thanks. But then I left with another manifesto to read! Universe!!!

The second meet, after much deliberation of all the reasons why no... I felt a nudge to consider why yes.

    Wè

        Wè

            Wè

Why not yes?

It's not every day the universe plants such a request on your path.

There must be a reason why I was here, even if I didn't understand, no matter how out of the box it all seemed.

And, what with all the fears? All the reasons why not good enough, not able enough, and the voice of "who do you think you are?"

What was there to lose?

What was there to gain?

Have you ever found yourself in a situation where everything screamed NO but your instinct suggested YES? Your heart warming to the prospect, daring you to trust the process…?

According to Michael A. Singer, author of *The Untethered Soul*, I had reached an 'edge'; a boundary to what I believed to be possible.

Every "wè, wè, wè", confirming my limiting beliefs, preconceived ideas about what is and what is not available to me — my background, my lack of knowledge, my lack of experience, my lack of everything.

On the surface those lacks appeared valid, but what about that I did have?

How about seeing how far this could take me?

What would it bring to enter into this unknown potential lion's den? You never know, it might be full of pussycats, purring at that which I had to offer.

The only person building a wall was me.

What if I dared to see...?

I could live without ever knowing, or I could simply find out.

Trembling, I decided to say yes. It was crazy, but I was going to say yes.

Yes to 'daring greatly'.

Yes to taking a leap.

Yes to trusting the net would appear.

Meeting number two

"The first thing I have to share is that the party needs to secure further funds, and we've decided to postpone putting forward a candidate."

"What?! But I came to say, yes!" I screamed in my head, but instead I listened silently and smiled whilst his voice faded into the distance and all I could hear and see in my mind's eye, was that **I was prepared to say YES!!**

Wè, wè, wè!

How about that?

The meeting, quickly and pleasantly over.

[gasp]

The moral of the story?

Do you believe the plan was to have me run as a candidate for Mayor of London?

Maybe...

Every now and again, life throws you a test.

A test to see how far you have come, to see if you dare step into a 'terrifying' unknown. A test of courage, confidence, curiosity.

This test shows up in relationships, career, work, life in general.

And it is a sign. It is a sign that you are ready for a growth spurt, to move beyond your comfort zone.

You may not know it consciously, but your soul knows.

And often all that's being asked of you is to say, yes, to 'feel the fear and do it anyway'. *(Susan Jeffers)*

Once you face your fears, once you stop laughing as I did and start feeling, seeing and believing... job done. You have passed the test. Moved through and beyond your edge.

There is no need to go further.

A yes/no turning point.

Taking a leap of faith, with no attachment to the result.

A lesson in surrender.

I often wonder what would have happened if I'd stayed in the space of 'no'. I would have wondered 'what if' — right?

But then again, sometimes you just have to commit to your decision and let things go, there is that too.

But I give thanks for the gift of this story.

It raised my confidence, increased my sense of self, brought me to a space I would never in a million years have thought I dare to enter.

Life **has** its plan.

You never know when a yes is going to help you grow. That's why daring to say yes in this case, was important no matter the butterflies of no.

I was never to enter into politics, there wasn't even the funding to do so. It was a matter of me saying yes and surrendering to the divine plan, the gift on offer.

I am sure you have your stories, times when you have conceded and times when you have not. It's all a learning curve, isn't it?

And one last thing…

Do you find yourself pigeoning opportunities as big or small?

Have you found that if something appears 'big' it brings more fear and if 'small' easy to do?

Big or small depends on your mindset, experiences, beliefs…

How about we together agree to reframe this big or small conditioning?

There is no big or small, there simply IS. Whatever it is, no big, no small, no "OMG, what, me??!!" Simply IS. Takes the pressure off and you become more ready to receive all gifts of life.

Wè, Wè, Wè!

Sa Cho, Sa Cho, Sa Cho!

"Because we are magical women
Born of magical women
We celebrate your magic"

- Pearl Cleage

We Speak Your Names

ACT 3   IN THE WINGS   SCENE 7

Ti Blackie

I am the daughter of Ti (pronounced Tee) Blackie
She who remains, faceless
and yet, her presence, ever felt

I am the daughter of Ti Blackie

In you I find strength

I am the daughter of Ti Blackie

Have yet to meet you in this life

Have chosen you to be my guide

Together we feel so alive!

I am the proud, great-granddaughter of
nwè, tèlman, nwè, é piti
Black, so, so black, and small
Powerful Ti Blackie

I kneel at your throne
invite you and all those who came before you
to join me on this road

Your power and strength
I forever uphold
Your spirit world so close to home
Ancestral change maker
Forever in the fold

Bless you
Ti Blackie

Ti Bo, Ti Bo
Kiss, Kiss

Inspired by the Edmund clan, the great-granddaughters of Ti Blackie, a sisterhood of strong black women with formidable flair.

My sister Celia; cousins Mary, Vav, Luna, Ya and Alix celebrate with love and pride our great-grandmother welcoming her into our joyful Patois Girls gatherings... "**I am the daughter of Ti Blackie you know!**" We pledge our inherited strength and resilience. And then together with our honorary Patois Girl sisters Christine, Gemma and Beverely, we fall about laughing!

Ti Blackie is believed to be Bajan born, of Barbados descent with long flowing hair. Arawak or Kalinago (Caribs)... the people of her heritage, unknown. According to our mothers, she was a petite and powerful soul. We love the energy of Ti Blackie. She keeps us 'whole'.

VIGNETTE - FEELING ALIVE!

Feeling Alive!

What a vibe...

I've got this feeling that tonight's gonna be a good night!

There are profound, positive changes popping inside —

I feel light,

My body full of might,

I am no longer weighted.

Feeling Alive!

What a vibe...

I've got this feeling that tonight's gonna be

A foot stomping, hip swinging, gloriously good night!

THE DANCE OF HAPPINESS

The dance of happiness is a beautiful thing,
I don't have to tell you what it brings.
We all know the nourishment of happiness,
The gift of this birthright
It doesn't take much to ignite
Forever ready to shine bright

The dance of happiness is a fabulous thing,
Makes your heart sing
La la!!!
A celebration of life
Where hearts unite,
Make no mistake,
This isn't blind faith.
Do whatever it takes
To inherit this blissful state,
The remedy of happiness,
That Superstar!

Jack of all Trades

There is nothing like finding your groove and then have someone pull the rug out from beneath you.

It started with a well-meant comment.

"Pearl, you do so much. You are a dancer, choreographer, teacher, director, a Homeopath, Neuro Linguistic Practitioner (NLP), a public speaker, you MC events... You do so much, I don't know where to place you. You can't possibly be an expert in any of these, I'd never book you... you are like a jack of all trades and master of none."

Well, that was like a punch to the gut. And from someone who loves me so. My 'dear friend' was concerned for me.

Who are you?

Where do you fit?

What exactly is your profession?

I felt winded, confused, surprised, hurt... Angry. And at that point, I knew it was time to take a deep breath, count to ten and step away.

Do you know when someone tugs at your emotions so acutely it can be because there is a level of truth lurking behind the scenes?

It could be in the form of a value, something very important to you or it can be an 'uglie'; a home truth waiting to be seen in full view — an opportunity as always for one's personal growth.

What was it in me she had touched?

I'd been on a spiritual path long enough to know that any rising negative emotions can reflect me. I may or may not like it, but there is always a clear message.

And so why the anger?

Other than, "how dare she?!"

After a deep, deep dive this is what I found...

Multi-passionate

I am a person who is excited by life and the curiosity of creativity.

If variety is the spice of life, as much I don't enjoy eating chilli, bring on the chilli! This is where I thrive.

As a dancer, I studied every style in both the contemporary and jazz field to experience all the different qualities of movement available to me.

I studied a Performance Arts degree as opposed to only dance because I wanted to experience the complete art of performance, yes as dancer, choreographer and also actor, singer, director, producer, theatre design, front of house, backstage management.

As for Homeopathy, I studied Practical Homeopathy as opposed to classical to incorporate within my practise, herbs, nutrition, flower essences, and much more.

NLP...? A palm reader told me to explore NLP. I had no idea what this was but when I looked into it, I realised I had been naturally practising NLP for much of my life. So, I chose to make it official with a qualification.

And as for public speaking and becoming President of The Professional Speaking Association within two years, it was my enthusiasm and of course talent that shone through.

I AM multi-passionate.

I AM multi- talented.

I AM eclectic, always working within multi-disciplines and I would not have it any other way.

So why angry?

All I had to do respond with all the above, but I didn't.

The Truth

In certain situations, social gatherings, networking, I'd dread the question 'so what do you do? Because there would be a list spurting from my lips with me rolling my eyes, as if apologising for the onslaught of words coming from my mouth.

Many a time I would silently wish I could be like others and state one thing only!

So, although I loved my multi-self, I was also at times embarrassed by her because she seemed so extreme and on 'the other side' of ... 'the norm'. Ouch!

And as for networking... well which version of me should I present today?! Anxiety was always in the background.

And so, my lovely friend's comment prodded the part of me that I'd been avoiding to face. The anger wasn't at her, the anger was at me, myself and I.

I had to admit at times I was being a traitor to myself by not fully believing. My indignant "how dare she?!" was a deflection.

And you know what, as I continued to face myself further, I became a miserable Charlie

(no offence to those named Charlie).

I became so disappointed in myself that this best described me...

Steptoe and Son

I became Steptoe

Of *Steptoe and Son* sitcom.

A complaining old grouch of a man.

Miserable, miserable

rag and bone stories of victimhood,

so pathetically sad.

My voice,

my tone ,

words clouded by internal soap operas.

Eastenders you'd love it here

I became Steptoe

of *Steptoe and Son* sitcom,

rattling, rust tainted misery.

Crazy how it creeps up on you

a slither here,

a ponder there,

with no real idea

until clear.

I become...who...?

Steptoe of...NO. STOP!!

This has had its time.

Today with a full moon

thank goodness for a full moon

new intention invitation.

I grab Steptoe of *Steptoe and Son*,

whizz him round,

boot him out the other way.

"No room for you here,

I have relinquished those rusty ideas!"

I wipe my brow.

Gosh laughable now,

how I became such a silly cow!

Renaissance Woman

I'm sitting in a café with friend Marsha — energy healer, reflexologist, stage designer and artist to boot! We are having a jack of all trade's conversation, and she says the magic words, "Pearl have you heard of the Renaissance Woman?" And THAT moment changed everything!

If you find yourself in a multi-passionate, thirst for life space, but with niggles attached, please investigate the **Renaissance Woman**. (Thank you, Marsha!)

> *"The concept of the Renaissance Woman has been around for centuries, and its relevance still holds true today. A Renaissance Woman is a woman who is a master of many trades, knowledgeable in a wide range of subjects, and a pursuer of diverse passions and pleasures. These women are visionaries, seamlessly weaving their multifaceted gifts and passions into a web of their unique expression. They are chameleons, brimming with creativity and innovation, with a flair for nuance. Embracing this concept isn't just beneficial, it's transformative — it unlocks your multidimensionality and allows the embodiment of your full potential."*
>
> - Jess, Renaissance Woman

Well, wot to say...?

I hyperventilate with excitement and recognition. All that time of struggle. If only I knew then what I knew now, but better late than never!

On her website, Jess expands on...

- Multidimensional skills
- Creativity and originality
- Independence and self-reliance
- How to lead as a Renaissance Woman
- Trust your intuition and multi-faceted nature
- Be willing to go first
- Embrace paradox
- Stimulate your dreams
- Become more empowered and fulfilled
- Prioritise community and connection
- Embrace beauty as a compass

'... remember and reclaim. Are you ready?'

JESS, I LOVE YOU!!!!!!!!!!!!!!! YES. I AM READY!!!

Oh, lawdy, lawd! The elaboration of each segment, of embracing your renaissance self; in fact the whole website mirrored me and my experiences to a T! Different expressions, but same context.

And as I continued to research the Renaissance Woman, I found there were many women who had **experienced**, **suffered** and **reclaimed** their multi-self; many who had walked that same walk, danced that bumpy dance.

I had found my community. I belonged.

No more need for shame, confusion and lone feelings as if something were wrong.

I felt empowered, uplifted, complete, strong.

If you are in this space, go find Jess, or a version of... I don't know Jess, but I know what it meant to find her, both for me and now for YOU.

Pearl, Author, Performer, Presenter, Holistic Health and Well-being Practitioner, Professional Speaker, Entrepreneur, Transformational Coach. I reclaim my modern-day Renaissance Woman. Yep. That will do me. Renaissance Woman is SHE.

The original comment I first received, as painful as it was at the time, lead to the great gift of both personal and professional clarity and acceptance. What more could I ask? Having made it through to the other end, I wouldn't have had it any other way, would you?

> *"Jack of all trades is a master of none, but oftentimes better than a master of one."*
>
> *- William Shakespeare*

It was interesting to learn this quote (as was with my friend) is often used as a criticism. However, in its entirety it is considered a *compliment*, yes, a compliment highlighting **versatility** of all things!

Well, what d'ya know...

Thank you.

Compliment accepted!

DANCE ALONG

'Cause you're free
To do what you want to do
You've got to live your life
Do what you want to do.

'Cause you're free
To do what you want to do
You've got to live your life
Do what you want to do.

- Ultra Naté

Mood II Swing

STRAIGHT LINES

I don't do straight lines,
I do curves and circles and free flowing lines.
I do lines that allow for expanse and freedom,
I do lines that appear to have no direction other than clear intent
and then, and only then, from that premise, do I arrive.

I do lines of adventure and openness,
lines that 'feel the fear and do it anyway'.
I do spaghetti, messy lines,
slurp them, fumble over them, not knowing them lines.
I don't do straight lines.

When straight calls for the easiest
most fun and direct lines,
of course I do straight lines;
but I keep an eye on them
in case they're old limiting lines,
tie me up in a mess lines,
Houdini strapped lines.
I no longer do them lines.

I refuse to,

away with you,

embracing only kite flying, ribboned lines.

A Tale of Three Augusts

August 2022

I feel good.
I believe this to be the year.
The year when I complete my book.
It's all go from here
But then I reach a blank.

All things go blank.
I meet people,
I agree to do things,
I offer to help others
and then, Blank.
Where has this come from?
It's as if I no longer know myself.

I appear to be functioning
but it looks as though I am not.
I am smiling,
Communicating,
I appear to be the same person
but... Blank.

Do I even know my name?

Blank

Blank

Blank!

It is frightening

Am I losing my mind?

It's as if I know nothing

I don't trust myself.

How can I...?

Who am I...?

What is going on?

I start to feel guilty for letting people down.

I say one thing and do the opposite

I am blank!!!

Everything I wished to do, achieve, has fallen by the wayside,
the blank cloud has tilted me to the side.

And the worst thing, is when I speak, I believe it, but then... Blank stupor!

I should share this with somebody,
but don't believe this to be the remedy.
Of course I don't,
I am not thinking clearly,
It's an awful place to be.

Eventually I wake up enough to visit my Homeopath.
She provides the healing remedies,
I angst about my plight.
I know she will do good by me.
The blank appears to shift,
the cloud begins to rise,
but not before the shame is well set inside.

There are many people I have not let in;
Rejected and they know not why.
Perhaps one day I will disclose the pain,
make amends,
and they may still be on my side.

I decide to enter a writing competition,
With every reason why 'no',
But the next day I am awakened from my dreams
the song *Welcome Home* by Peters and Lee,
it is playing wistfully.
A favourite of my parents,
I imagine them swaying and stepping a hip swinging
1, 2, 1, 2, 3 and singing at the top of their voices.
It brings a smile...

Welcome home
[sing along]
Welcome
Come on in, and close the door
You've been gone, too long
Welcome,
you're home once more...

Perhaps it is symbolic of having been 'away' (blank) and now, returning 'home'...?

Fingers crossed,

I shrug in hope,

please let me be on route 'home'.

August 2023

This is the month.

I know it is.

To complete book-baby.

I have set the time aside.

Let's do this.

We can do this.

The book has a plan,

Surrender to the plan.

Who am I to believe I know?

What do I know...?

Me, in charge of the timeline?

Best to let go.

August 2022 it was to be
Now 2023, let us see...
Come on, we can do this!!!

AUGUST 2023 came and went.
No matter how hard I tried
there seemed to be a reason,
a stalling mechanism in my 'drive'.
It's not that I wasn't committed or determined
it simply wouldn't let 'be'

Book-baby, come on we can do this,
Come on, Can we do this...?
Certainly!
But then, nothing could have prepared me...

Trauma

Stole four months of my life.
The grief is ad infinitum.

Slowly, slowly, does it
no pushing, pulling, no avoiding, no rushing,
slowly, slowly, does it
To heal

I long for my recovery,
I long to be the person I once was.
But she is no longer

what I once knew, is now dead, that's for sure
my trust in life, is at the foot of the door.

Slowly, slowly, lovingly, patiently, kindly does it
to heal the wounds that feel so sore,
feeling broken and scattered across the floor.

There is a bigger picture though, you can explore…
The drama of life, knocking at your door
The movie of your soul, being at the core.
Past life agreements, contracts,
forgotten handshakes, karma, ancestral weaving,
all of it, scenes of your soul's journey,
it being at the fore.
The trauma is accurate in all its forms.
Friend or foe?
In due course, you will know.
Trauma, you stole four months of my life,
and the grief is ad infinitum
but freedom requires I get out of my head,
drop back into my heart,
trust in my soul's knowing
for there is the new start.

Power to face
Power to accept

Slowly, slowly, lovingly, patiently, kindly does it

The wounds that feel so sore
becoming less more.

Letting in the light
A flicker of light
I may even hit the dance floor.

The death of three loved ones within weeks, flying free. It took the wind out of my sails, placing trauma deep within me.

I am so thankful book-baby for having resisted me, there is no way I could have handled your publicity.

Grief, I know you well my old friend, no arguing, I surrender and take a pause, accept life, death, rebirth thoughts.

Knowing the gift of time will soon heal all.

One Love

> "The paradox of trauma. In order to heal you need to remember. But in order to survive, you need to forget."
>
> - Rachel Matlow, Dead Mom Walking

There was nothing else for it but to step aside, take the bumpy ride, until...

August 2022 it was to be

Then 2023

Now 2024

Let's see...

Delete

"Sometimes you've just got to purge"

I heard me say it,
I felt it so true,
It scared me but I had the deepest sense it was what I had to do.

Easing gently through my grief
I could feel a swirl beckoning me,
Allowing for something fresh and new.
Grief as always bringing a promise,
A wave of renewal.

I started revisiting my book
But it felt stuck and trapped
As if in a web of the past mishaps.

What once felt liberating and joyful to explore,

My writing now considered an absolute bore.

"So last year."

Too much had changed.

It was time to declutter, clean, clear, cancel,

To dust off the old chat,
Life's lessons had seen to that.

Now to honour only where I was truthfully at.

I felt the need to shed skin
But crazy, right...?
What a thought.
To start over...??
Crazy...?!
But I had no energy to dance across the floor.

The decision however was not mine...

DELETE

'By accident' of course, I deleted all the documents on my laptop. AND I emptied the trash!! HELP!!!!!

The short version is that there was no help to be had. Every recent document, file of the past few years, all of it gone never to be restored, including... my book!!

Why did I do that?! It wasn't intentional... it really wasn't, **it — really — wasn't** but somehow... Oh lordy lord, how could I have been so...? Grrrrr, really Pearl!!! Who does that..?!!! Stupid 'Cloud' — don't even understand The Cloud, but now I know it to be a mirror of my files so delete files and then delete the trash, despite the flash of a warning well there you have it, DELETE!!!

Recently I had been crying in my dreams.

I wondered why, thought it grief in the silence of my mind.

But now, with this, this inexcusable error (she still in oh so denial) after a few days of panic and hyperventilating, even she had to admit, to stop the pretence of not knowing deep within her soul, it was clearly, the only way, for her to roll.

"Do you know butterflies rest when it rains
because the rain damages their wings?
It's ok to rest during life's storms
you'll fly again once they're over."

- Source Unknown

August 2024

YOU came to me as quick as a flash.

You woke me from my dreams,

I caught the image of you,

but what did you mean?

I thought you to be 2022, then 2023

but 2024 is when you chose to be.

Sleeves rolled up

Time for renewed action

Pen at the ready.

The planets and stars appear aligned

Transporting my destiny

Providing strength and energy

To birth Book-Baby!

At last labour free

Announced for all to see

And so, it was meant to be... **August 2024**

What a journey...

The three steps of August, as if the three stages of labour, with one final push!

Contracting and **releasing**

contracting and **releasing**

contracting and **releasing!**

Book-baby may have appeared well overdue, but her timing was imperfectly perfect. It was imperative to be so, to birth completely refreshed and renewed.

I WILL RISE

It's through your wounds that the light gets in
It's in the darkest rooms that the candle glows
It's at the bottom of your deepest well
That the softest earth will break your fall

It's on the mountain that I learned the most
It's when I fell down, that I knew my strength
It's not my mistakes, tell you who I am
It's what I do with them and who I will become.

And I will rise like a poor child given a chance.
And I will rise like the sunup through the clouds
And I will rise, every time that I sing
And when I fall, I'll fall gracefully.
cause when I fall, I am given wings...

- Lucinda Drayton
The Road Least Travelled

WHERE DO I BEGIN?

Where do I begin
To tell the story of how great a love can be
The sweet love story that is older than the sea
The simple truth about the love she brings to me
Where do I start?
- Andy Williams

Where do I begin
The Rose Quartz Story and the love she brought to me
That sweet love story, the dance of life 'it' being key
The Truth of which is yours if you permit to see
Where do I start?

Where do I begin
The forest of legs jigging manifestly
The little girl dancing hid her true identity
No running away could erase her souls' destiny
Where do I start?

It fills my heart to see how far she's come
She plays chase and laughs
With mum has so much fun
All pain dissolved
The hurts absolved.

And now they both dance free
With love and sovereignty
Peace at last
One heart of unity
Their healed embrace
Abound with Grace.

Where do I begin
To tell the story of how great self-love can be
The sweet love story of divine serenity
The simple truth that life is all its meant to be?

Where do I start?

Perhaps with heart
My Precious Heart...

How about your precious heart.
Where does it begin?

WINGS

Where are you holding back?

Where are you not allowing yourself to take that leap and be all you can be?

Where are you playing it safe?

You have wings.

Trust that you will be held and supported.

It is time to be open to them,

take that leap and fly.

- Tara Jackson

Embodied Wisdom Oracle Deck

GLOW

Wherever you go
Tune into your glow
For you are your light
Always of the Light
And now it is time to
Glow, Glow, Glow!

IN THE WINGS: A VISUALISATION

Imagine yourself standing in the wings about to enter centre stage
stage right or stage left,
upstage or down.

You choose, for this is ALL about YOU
The world awaits you and has taken its seat.

Lights, Camera. Action.

The music starts or perhaps you choose to enter in silence
either way, you take that first step.

Any hesitation… anxiety…?
remember, **this** is your moment
you have cleared your path to be here;
spent hours, days, weeks, years in the rehearsal studio of your life.

You are ready.

You name that feeling, the flutter of fear that it is
and thank it for showing you who you used to be.
But now, now you are **becoming**
and walk on stage, dignified.

You reach centre stage,
You can hear a pin drop,

Complete silence in reverence of you.

Click
Spotlight, circling round.

You stand
Certain,
Capable,
Confident,
growing ten feet tall and more.

You gaze out into the world
and the world looks back at you
all eyes on you
not a flicker, as you stand, steadily strong.

Heat rising,
here she comes…
an energy that emanates all the beautiful 'self's
self-love, self-approval, self-esteem, self-respect, self-acceptance, all well overdue.
Every part of you, your sentient being, explosively alive, full, complete.

And then… and only then
When you are ready
You…

Turn to exit
holding your dance steadily, proudly within.
For she is **yours**,
SHE is your personal Glow.

You move to exit in your power, strength and... (over to you dear reader, what else comes to mind...?)

Your 'épaulement' a shoulder movement, arm extending leading proud, head held high.

You silently sing... *"sisters are doing it for themselves"*,
your rhythm reclaimed.
The spotlight follows you towards off stage, shining your path
and as you reach the wings to finally exit,
the world leaps to its feet,
full of applause
spellbound broken

Encore, Encore, Encore!

You turn, suddenly, now eagle-winged ballerina in flight
twirling, swirling
your feet light and air-filled
you leap, jeté across the stage floor
soaring through time and space
you land
steady
still

powerfully.

You pause
take a bow,
receive
welcome
appreciate.

You have found your ground,
solid in your inner knowing
that from here on in
encore or not

you ~ have ~ arrived.

FULL CIRCLE

[Voiceover]

Who would have thought, who would have guessed that The Wish could have opened so many doors?

The little girl surrounded by a forest of legs no longer hiding and ready for what's next.

She now contented and full of glee, it's hard to believe this shero was once on her knees.

But that was then, this is now, her healing steps have shown her how.

INNER CHILD PEACE

I will be her calm

A picture of her ease

As I move through life

A child of inner peace

CURTAIN CALL

"Be happy and free, live your life"

- Regina

A New Dawn...

GET HAPPY

Forget your troubles, c'mon get happy
You better chase all your cares away

Shout "hallelujah", c'mon get happy
Get ready for the judgement day
The sun is shinin', c'mon get happy
The Lord is waiting to take your hand
Shout "hallelujah", c'mon get happy
We're going to the promise land...

- Judy Garland

[BLACK OUT]

FOYER CHIT-CHAT

What does *Dancing to the Rhythm of Your Life* say to you?

Adrienne Robertson

Acceptance and celebration of your individual uniqueness, the winding road of authenticity

Andréa Watts

A metaphor that, for me means having the freedom, creativity, courage and wisdom to live my life joyously and authentically with flow and ease... recognition of different seasons, tempos and that the rhythms change and being aligned to that. It's a powerful title because it does hold so much... movement, trust, intuition, connection.

It is so deep...

Antonia Adenji

To me it invokes the underlying rhythms and patterns that move and stir beneath the surface of our conscious mind. When we learn to tap into them, embrace and accept them, we are in our flow and can experience the range of possibilities that life offers.

Dancing with those experiences suggests being in connection with the Divine and a connection with joy.

Bridget Blossom

What it means to me is becoming authentic in a fun way... becoming authentic can be hard work in psychological terms maybe, so I'm dying to read the book to see how to dance it!

Cate Jordan-Dunne
Allow yourself to shine

Celia Simpson
No matter what, you will always come through.. .just believe in yourself!

Ceryn Rowntree
Moving in flow with what's true to me;
the real, deep, wise and powerful me, in every second.

Fast or slow, up or down, wild or graceful

There is no right or wrong way

As long as I always come back to the rhythm that is mine.

Dainei Tracy
Being in relationship with everything that arises, to any beat of existence.

Della Murad
Life isn't about perfection; it's about feeling, expression and presence.
This is what dancing says to me.

Elaine Grant
Free movement through life, physical and spiritual freedom
Dancing to my own tune I can set my own pace of how I want to live my life.

Eve Oliveira
Tune into my inner DJ, to listen to the music that is playing and to go with
the flow, not trying to fit into certain rhythms,
not trying to dance dances that don't really speak to me.

Just go for it!

Gemma Pacquette

The title captures the essence of life in any direction.

Jan Sumner-Rivers

The breaking, vibrant, dancing wave is you in dance changing your being into a joyful movement of glorious possibility.

Jane Charity

We can either breathe through what life brings or stop breathing. Bend like a daisy but keep your roots deep.

Jeanefer Jean-Charles

To me it simply means, 'recognising who you are and taking charge of your journey in life — no matter what.

Jennifer Silverton

It's finding the rhythm that's hard and changing to a new rhythm when your life changes around you. That's what I am doing now!

Jenny Tryfonos

As Erma Bombeck once said, "when I stand before God at the end of my life, I would hope that I would not have a single bit of talent left and I could say I've used everything that you gave me", and that's the essence of the book, celebrating who you are and everything you stand for. Living your best life.

Jo Short

Conjures up images and thoughts of someone physically responding to life's journey, embracing it and moving with it musically, and with a smile.

Judith Palmer

I love the title... It brings to my mind a song by Tarrus Riley, She's Royal. There is a line "the way she moves to her own beat" and so to me it means... I move to my own beat.

I do what I want, when I want, how I want.

June Gamble

Listening to and trusting my inner wisdom that guides me to be still or take conviction as I navigate the various stages of my life.

Lisa Glydon

I get nervous about dancing...

but your title makes me think it doesn't matter what you are, where you are, how comfortable you are with dance. In fact it's not really about dance,

it's about being in tune with yourself and in tune with your rhythm of life.

Accept yourself and go forward with dance in your spirit!

Lorraine Pannetier

Dancing to the Rhythm of your Life, to me it means following your own path, choosing to align life, work and love to your own inner truth. When you live this way, you'll flow with the current rather than hitting waves!

Lucinda Drayton

For me this speaks of acceptance and flow. Loving who I am as I am. Accepting the challenges that must come towards me and through this learning to dance with life as I grow and learn.

Luna Mathurin

Just getting on with it, staying positive, enjoying and doing your best as you go through your daily life.

Marsha Roddy

It says to me, the freedom to follow your path, in a joyous way.

Dancing = joy   Rhythm = our path

Martha Stylianou

I can control the narrative of how I live my life.

I might just need help getting there...

Masana De Souza

Dancing to the rhythm of my life means I am engaging my open Heart and mind, and allowing my spiritual essence to be revealed in each moment in an exquisite flow of love and pure Intention.

Maxine Bell

For me it means riding all the different waves of all things that happen good and bad, like learning how to step into whatever happens. It's not about controlling your life, it's about resilience and dancing with each step, wherever that rhythm takes you... finding a way to move through the ups and downs of life.

Nina Buchanan

An opportunity to create Utopia

through going beyond the illusions of living an ordinary life.

Rachel Priestman

I really resonate with the title. Love it!

Sharon O'Regan

Being in tune with all that is.

Theresa Beattie
The sense of looking at and gaining joy from the familiar after time away.

Vav Mathurin
The title says highs and lows... lows and highs.

Vicki Igbokwe-Ozoagu
To me it means feeling freedom and lightness in my life.

Ya
To me the title says ONE ACCORD!

And... YOU...

Bravo!

I Am One
We Are One

Now to dance to your ROYL...

An Audience With... Pearl

Congratulations

Thank you

So glad you overcame your writing fears to create this amazing book.

Thank you

So how were you able to do that, overcome that fear...?

To be honest it was that moment when I felt the nausea of fear that I knew I was in trouble. That moment when I saw the social media post from Nicola Humber to join her Writing Mastermind. As I read it, I immediately felt this tremor and I thought oh my goodness, this is crazy... how much longer do I hold onto these writing fears? This is ridiculous, I am so fed up of this learnt limiting belief. Every dissertation, during my degree, Homeopathic or NLP training, every epic writing situation I would become a mess. No. It had to stop. And so "yes", as I've said many a time during the book, it gets to a stage where you say enough is enough and make the decision to move towards that which is holding you victim. The tremors indicated that joining the writing mastermind would be the answer.

Tell us more...

It was the time of the Pandemic. There was a lot of collective fear and I knew this was intensifying my response; everything was heightened, right? I wanted to release the load, and the Unbound Writing Mastermind — note that word 'unbound' — that was to be the space for me. A space of creative freedom where no rules rule, where I didn't have to worry about grammar or spelling; a space of exploratory writing and adventure with the only rule being that you remain true to yourself throughout. An unbound community, encouraging your unbound self to be free both on paper and in life! What was there not to join?!

If being in such a supportive environment didn't help me overcome all the writing barriers, nowhere would. Some days, I howled because of the pain of the resistances and the changes I was demanding of myself. Other days I would sing and dance. It was all acceptable. I was acceptable. Each and every one of us acceptable. No judgements, criticisms, pure encouragement, one heck of a healing space.

By the way, I had no intentions of writing a book.

Really...?

No. If and when a book happened to come calling, all well and good, but at no stage was there pressure to do so. That too made a difference to my writing commitment. I wrote for me and my healing only.

Joining the mastermind was an extension of my 'morning pages'; a form of journalling I had been practising, inspired by Julia Cameron's book *The Artist's Way — A Course in Discovering and Recovering Your Creative Self.* So, between the two, my writing was nurtured holistically, you could say, in two practices of creative freedom.

Great. And so at what stage did you decide to write a book?

I have no idea when I decided to write a book, it just sort of fell into place. In fact, what was in place was a title and the book being a live performance. I was clearly shown during meditation me walking on stage waving to a large crowd, all of us excited by the anticipation of exploring the book's themes, dancing, singing, going deep into reflection, holding conversations that connected us as One. I was even given an anthem during my dreams. Clearly there was a Divine plan and my role was to follow lead.

Interesting. OK, now let's talk the style of your book... Did you plan it this way...?

Goodness me, no. I am in awe of the book and the creative, innovative way she chose to show up!

What I would say is the first thing I did was to get every initial idea out of my head and sprawled across a bedroom wall — the threads I wished to follow, different themes, potential journeys... I considered the who, the what, the whys, the obstacles. I drew mind-maps, story boards, all directing to the message of the book.

The style however, I thought it would be linear storytelling from A to Z. But no, my jazz hands did the writing! Syncopated in every way. Ad hoc, stories, ideas, songs etc surprising me all the way. Maybe it is because I often had music on in the background or often jumped up and danced to bring more energy to the writing... perhaps this inspired the work, who knows...? I do love the way, 'she' is so rhythmical and can't wait to create the audio version. I have the direction all planned!

[Lol!] Of course you have...well, we look forward to the audio version too.

What is your biggest learning?

In three words: faith, trust and surrender. I found the process of writing tested all that I thought I knew about yourself. Any fixed ideas were crushed, thrown out, a demand that I let go of all things old and surrender to the new ways of creation being 'asked' of me now. Nothing else would do. And when I resisted and dared not trust the process, it's as if my pen would stop the writing and refuse to go any further.

By the way, did I mention the spirit of my book, Serafina–Bookina?

No...?

Well, very early on in the writing process Nicola encourages you to connect to the spirit of your book. This I thought hilarious but hey, who was I not to play? Serafina-Bookina soon made herself known and with her no-nonsense loving attitude, made it clear that she was in charge; she would lead me to the pre-destined destination, should I allow it.

Serafina-Bookina and my authentic inner voice, I soon came to realise were united as one. When I stepped away from 'her' I was stepping away from my truth. So, I listened and grew closer to my heart.

Wow, that is powerful stuff and a bit 'out there' if you don't mind me saying...?

Not at all. It is. [Lol!]

Any struggles?

The battles I faced between self-belief and self-doubt were huge.

Who was I to believe I could write a book?

Where do I begin?

Do I have what it takes to engage with the reader... translate my performer /audience skills into a book writing form... Could I do it?

When ACT I was complete, it felt as though that was it, the book done. What else could I possibly say...?

ACT II, was so different from ACT I. Does it even make sense...?

ACT III, well that took weeks, months of gathering away from the book, no pen to paper until its 'voice' finally landed.

Oh, the list is endless!

Thank goodness for my daily spiritual practice, this held me steady. I leaned into my faith in God, not the conventional, fear inducing, guilty version, but the divine, mother-father of highest love, support, nurture, nature, guidance. I leaned into my faith big time, surrendering to my highest good, doing my best to trust the process. This book-baby writing journey brought every opportunity to deepen and ground into faith, trust and surrender... my personal growth, right...? Walking the talk.

On that note, what about the person who feels they have two left feet, would love to dance to the rhythm of their life, but has no idea where to start?

What I've found is when you say "yes" to change and make a commitment to transforming areas of your life, the answers soon do appear. You may have to show up in your vulnerability to let others know you are seeking help; but before you know it, there will be someone who knows someone or something to help you on your way. The universe will support you. And of course, there is The ROYL Tour!

Yes, a nice segue into what's next...?

Next in line is Author Pearl Jordan and The ROYL Tour! Dancing to the Rhythm Of Your Life in action. We will be offering many services of support, through coaching, workshops, courses, retreats, so I'd advise you join the mailing list to be kept in the loop of what's next. And of course I can be contacted directly, my details are within the resources section of the book.

Hmmmm... nice one! Might there also be another book planned?

One step at a time please!!! [Lol!]

Ok. A final word...

I love Kaypacha's Mantra...

"When I shine my light into the dark, I don't know what to expect, but only by sharing my deepest self, can I truly be fully met."

This is the ROYL Tour! Helping people like you dance your light into the dark, following the beam to your wonderful, powerful, magical, introvert, extrovert, authentic, love-full, vulnerable, sovereign self... allowing yourself to be fully met. Recovering, discovering, honouring your intimate story, your new chapter, in the wings, your dot, dot, dot...

Thank you, Pearl. That's all we have time for. It's been great to hear of your process' and the journey of birthing your, as you call her... book-baby.

We wish you every success as you gift her out into the world.

Thank you.

The pleasure was mine.

See you all on The ROYL Tour!!

[CURTAINS CLOSE]

APPLAUSE!!

It takes a village

A BIG round of applause to all my inner circle of family and friends, my 'corps de ballet'. Thank you for providing a perfect backdrop of love, support and encouragement. I have so appreciated you cheering me on, and your fan-club enthusiasm has certainly helped me dance over the finishing line.

Our 'dancing and singing' together, the conversations, explorations, your advice and wisdom so essential and tantamount to this book writing journey and my healing recovery... through you I have remedied much.

The APPLAUSE is yours. You know who you are...

Sending much Love and Gratitude.

Please take a bow!

TD, (Tommy Dunne) Querido, we danced together in our youth and have continued to dance through life. Thank you for being a perfect partner, ever present, and for keeping me nourished and fed during this book writing epic.

Liam and Michael, from a mother with great pride, not only do you 'Candy' with me on the dance floor, but you are 'busting some serious moves' on the stage of life. Keep on thriving.

Nora, Gorgeous, thank you for bringing the deepest, warmest smile into my life.

Bullies, my dance in life buddies — Martha Stylianou, Jeanefer Jean-Charles, Leon Hazlewood and Vik Sivalingam, Cake. Pudding. Dessert. Need I say more...? Thank you!

Patois Girls, J'Lucians, WAC Girlies, PALs, Charlie's Angels, Sistren Solidarity Circle, Foyer Chit-Chat Queens, too many to mention individually, please know that you are being celebrated, and I thank you for your sisterhood of love and deep binding friendship.

Healing Lovelies, Les and Janet, past, present, future as one, healing all aspects of me and my family... Thank you for your generosity, guidance and the laughter.

Lorraine Pannetier, my book writing buddy, you tuned into my rhythm with such lyrical ease. Thank you for always bringing a zing to my step and congratulations on your *Raising Wild Birds* book release.

Dainei Tracy, you welcomed me into your home, we created our writing retreat. Thank you for providing a leap into my writing commitment. I am waiting for the release of your book, eagerly.

Brahma Kumaris Family, your spiritual sustenance, love and friendship provides the wind beneath my wings.

Andréa Watts, you raise me up! Thank you for the *coaching with collage* creations that have shone a light, guiding me... Together we climb great mountains.

Carole Ann Rice let's continue to create magic in Kew.

Jenny Tryfonos, Angel, Heaven sent... Thank you.

Lucinda Drayton, singing our hearts out and dancing our socks off, united all the way.

Maxine Bell... 'Dance as light as a feather with feet barely touching the ground' the healing power of dance unites us; your beautiful poem ignites the dance within unbound.

A Resounding Encore to my Reading Cheerleaders

Jeanefer Jean-Charles MBE
Antonia Adenji
June Gamble
Jo Short
Mal Peachey
Marie McCluskey MBE
Mike Blissett
Theresa Beattie OBE
Simone Frazier
Vicki Igbokwe-Ozoagu
Yaba Badoe

In your unique way each one of you brought the guidance and clarity I so needed to keep me on track and confidently moving forwards. Be it through hours of editing, listening, or your gentle, honest non-judgemental feedback, you had me see what there was to see and make amends where necessary. Together you helped me find my writing groove. THANK YOU!!

Roll the drums Credits

Martha Stylianou and Màire (Moy) Clerkin — you held me and helped me to have the confidence to keep on going. I don't know how I would have completed this book without you and for that I am truly grateful. To have your creative eye and expertise in the space with me, made all the difference! Thank you my creative buddies, for dancing on paper with me, all the way.

Nicola Humber — Publisher, Unbound Press, we tingled when we first met, and here we are... Thank you for guiding me to transform my life beyond measure and for your encouragement to dare to believe that I could be an author. Words cannot express the gratitude I feel. I am in awe of the magic you create by supremely being you, and for your Unbound Community, where sisters are daring to do it for themselves. Together we rise, and I love you for it! Thank you for the opportunity. Thanks to all the Unbound Women who held me tight over the past few years, helping me to achieve this enormous book writing milestone. I thank you Nicola for the waves of movement and dance we are about to create!

Ceryn Rowntree — Editor, I could never have imagined you would be the chosen one to dance through the pages of Book-Baby with me. My heart overflows with the wonder and the miracle of it all. Who would have thought that an introduction would lead to us being here together, dancing lyrical with words? The universe clearly had a plan. Thank you for your enthusiastic guidance and the deep, reassuring clarity you provided. I am so 'lucky, lucky, lucky' to have your beautiful spirit forever engraved throughout the message of these pages.

The Unbound Team — Magnificent duo Emma (Em) Mulholland and designer Lynda Mangoro, you have been the most perfect birthing partners. Thank you for such a dedicated, pain free book production labour of **LOVE**!

Serafina Bookina — Spirit of Book-baby, you announced yourself unapologetically, full of zest, energy and non-negotiable, sleeves rolled up, "let's get this job done". You humoured my doubting moments, rolled your eyes when I threw many a hissy fit, you painted your nails whilst waiting patiently for me to get over myself and you boogied with joy when I reached a high! Thank you for choosing me to birth book-baby, such a gift to present to the world. You are the STAR in action.

And last but not least...

Moses and Regina — I couldn't have done this without you. You brought me life. You helped me 'produce' my story. In you I witnessed undeterred strength, focus, determination, self- respect, self-esteem and cultural pride – great qualities to pass on down the line. You also taught me that we are imperfect, all doing our best to 'be' and to thrive; there are no stones to be thrown at others, for "There by the grace of the Divine go I".

The dance of life is a powerful and intricate thing, once you fully embrace this, LOVE can you bring. We danced many a dance throughout our lives, peace and acceptance is the presence that today unites.

I dedicate this **final applause to you...**

"Sealed With A Kiss"

GLOSSARY

ACT I

Overture: Musical instrumental introduction

Voice Over: Voice of an unseen commentator

Welcome

Boogie Back: Lindy Hop Swing Jazz — a syncopated dance step backwards

Ali Shuffle: Mohammed Ali, famous boxer, renowned for his fast footwork

Scene 1

Marianne Williamson: American author, speaker and political activist

Raja Yoga Meditation: Brahma Kumaris World Spiritual University

Inner Child: Carl Jung, a prominent psychologist introduced the concept of the "inner child" as a part of the unconscious mind representing childhood experiences and emotions that influence behaviours, thoughts and feelings in adulthood.

Scene 2

Shirley Temple: American Child Star, Actress, Singer

Pirouette: 360 degrees turn on one foot.

Weekend Arts College: (WAC) set up in 1978, a pioneering performing arts centre offering high quality classes in dance, drama and music, taught by working professionals to young aspiring students from a diverse background both economic and cultural.

En pointe: Dancing on your toes

Scene 3

West Side Story (1961): Directed by Robert Wise and Jerome Robbins. Written by Ernest Lehman. Music by Leonard Bernstein

ACT II

Scene 1

No mistakes can be made... Jim Jarmusch, American Film Director, Screen Writer and Musician

The work of rehearsal... Peter Brook, English theatre and Film Director

Scene 4

Cakewalk: A promenade or march of African American origin, in which the couples with the most intricate steps received cakes as prizes

Kiss their teeth: Sucking air through teeth with attitude to show disapproval

Royal Variety Show: An annual televised stage variety show to raise money for royal charities attended by members of the Royal Family

Kylie Minogue: Australian singer, songwriter, actress

Scene 5

Martha Graham: American modern dancer, teacher, choreographer whose style, the Graham technique, transformed Modern dance.

Scene 6

SOS: Inspired by the Positive Thinking Course — Brahma Kumaris, Women led Worldwide Spiritual Organisation dedicated to personal transformation and world peace.

Scene 8

Columbo: American Detective TV series 1971-1978 NBC

Scene 9

Wings: Space off stage where performer stands unseen to enter and exit

Cyclorama (Cyc): A large, backdrop screen used in theatre, film

Corpse: To spoil a piece of theatre by either freezing, forgetting words, or laughing on stage

Scene 13

Jazz dance is a clown amongst the arts: The Anthology of American Jazz Dance by Gus Giordano, where the author proves the opposite.

Tread the Boards: Perform on stage

Scene 19

Feeling Great No Matter What: Brahma Kumaris Production, Hammersmith Apollo, London, August 2010

Scene 21

Dorothy Dandridge: American Actress Singer

Harry Belafonte: American Actor, Singer, Civil Rights Activist

ACT III

Scene 1

The Wings: Exit and entrance areas just off stage where performers stand unseen by the audience.

Scene 2

Gaze afar: Lindy Hop Swing Dance step

A Bridge

One finger one thumb: A Nursery Rhyme

Scene 4

Click: A swear word alternative created by Regina and her Edmund sisters.

Black Lives Matter: In 2013, activists and friends Alicia Garza, Patrisse Cullors, and Ayọ Tometi originated the hashtag #BlackLivesMatter on social media following the shooting of African-American teen Trayvon Martin.

Scene 6

Daring Greatly: Brené Brown, author, researcher and storyteller

Scene 7

Arawaks/ Kalinago: The Arawaks were the first known inhabitants of Saint Lucia. The Kalinago, commonly known as the Caribs, invaded and conquered the island in AD 800.

J. Jean-Charles *Patwa / Patois* dance project. Research briefing paper. Hassan Mahamdallie Feb 2024

Scene 8

Steptoe and Son: British Hit Comedy Series starring Harry H Corbett and Wilfrid Brambel

Eastenders: British Soap Drama

Scene 9

Epaulement: French Ballet term — shoulder and arm leading forward with spinal rotation of the torso.

RESOURCES

THE ROYL TOUR!

You can find Pearl on The **ROYL** (Rhythm of Your Life) **Tour!**

For the latest news, updates - retreats, workshops, to invite Pearl to speak at your event or book club – for a free sign-up newsletter/book mailing list, pre-orders/Early Bird Bonus, go to: www.pearljordan.com/author

Film:

Bullies Ballerinas — *Barefeet and Crazy Legs* film plus interviews: 1996 Arts Council Of England Award Winner

https://www.youtube.com/watch?v=IBQPAZObgYg

Hellzapoppin' (1941) for the greatest and most inspiring Lindy Hop Swing sequence ever filmed, featuring the original creators of the Lindy Hop, Whitey's Lindy Hoppers.

https://www.youtube.com/watch?v=ahoJReiCaPk

West Side Story Dance Scenes

America

https://www.youtube.com/watch?v=YhSKk-cvblc

Dance At The Gym

https://www.youtube.com/watch?v=1u9CAaxMKWY

Cool

https://www.youtube.com/watch?v=hMMAB3MNCKw

Theatre:
The 'Patois' Dance Tour: www.jeanefer.com

Raja Yoga Meditation:
https://www.brahmakumaris.org
https://www.globalcooperationhouse.org
http://www.just-a-minute.org

Oracle Deck Cards:
Embodied Wisdom Oracle Deck, Tara Jackson
Strange Grace Journey Deck, Jennifer Mayol
Goddess Guidance Oracle Cards, Doreen Virtue, PhD, 2003

MUSIC CATALOGUE

 **The ROYL Music Playlist:**
https://open.spotify.com/playlist/5XazuLEUtiHeYArQ3BFrih?si=2d4a8031546148c5

ACT I

Song: **Shackles (Praise You)**
Songwriters: E. Atkins-Campbell, T. Atkins-Campbell, W. Campbell
Artist: Mary. Mary

Welcome

Lyric: *Joy and pain like sunshine and rain*
Song: **Joy and Pain**
Singer/Songwriter: Frankie Beverly
Artist: Maze

Scene 1

Lyric: *What is this thing called love...*
Song: **What is this thing called love**
Songwriter: Cole Porter
Artist: Ella Fitzgerald — 'Queen of Jazz'

Song: **A Hundred Thousand Angels**
Songwriters: Lucinda Drayton, Andy Blissett (Bliss)
Artist: Lucinda Drayton

Scene 2

Lyric: *I feel good...*

Song: **I Got You (I Feel Good)**
Songwriter: Theron Thomas
Artist: James Brown

Song: **Running Away**
Songwriter: Frankie Beverly
Artists: Frankie Beverly, Maze

Lyric: *Enough is enough...*

Song: **No More Tears**
Songwriters: Bruce Roberts, Paul Jabara
Artists: Donna Summer, Barbara Streisand

Song: **Let Me Love You**
Songwriter: Bunny Mack
Artist: Bunny Mack

Scene 8

Song: **I Am Blessed**
Songwriter: Not known
Artist: Mr Vegas

ACT II
Overture

Song: **Fame**
Songwriters: Dean Pitchford, Michael Gore
Artist: Irene Cara

Scene 16

Song: **Here Comes The Sun**

Songwriter: George Harrison

Artist: The Beatles

Scene 17

Lyric: *Feeling Hot, Hot, Hot*

Song: **Hot Hot Hot**

Songwriter: Alphonsus Cassell

Artist: Arrow

Scene 18

Song: **Kung Fu Fighting**

Singer/Songwriter: Carl Douglas

Song: **I Can See Clearly Now**

Songwriter: Johnny Nash

Artist: Jimmy Cliff

Scene 19

Lyric: *Pack up your weakness...*

Song: **Road of Gold**

Songwriters: Lucinda Drayton and Andy Blissett

Artist: Lucinda Drayton

Scene 21

Lyric: *Beat out dat rhythm on a drum*

Song: **Beat Out Dat Rhythm On a Drum, Act II**

Lyric: *The cards don't lie*

Song: **De Cards don' lie**

Musical: Carmen Jones
Composer: Georges Bizet, Oscar Hammerstein II
Conductor: Henry Lewis
Artists: W. Fernandez / S. Benson/ D. Evans / M. Austin / G. Baker plus additional cast

ACT III
Overture
Song: **Coming Home**
Singer/Songwriter: Jenny Plant

A Bridge
Song: **One Finger One Thumb**
Songwriters: Bram Morrison, Lois Ada Lillienstein, Sharon Hanson
Artist: The Wiggles

Scene 4
Song: **Walk With Us – For Black Lives Matter**
Composer: Alexis Ffrench
Artist: Alexis Ffrench

Scene 5
Lyric: *At first, I was afraid I was petrified*
Song: **I Will Survive**
Songwriters: Freddie Perren, Dino Fekaris
Artist: Gloria Gaynor

Lyric: *Just my imagination running away with me*
Song: **Just my Imagination**
Songwriters: Norman Whitfield and Barratt Strong
Artists: The Temptations

Scene 7

Lyric: *I've got this feeling that tonight's gonna be a good night!*

Song: **I Gotta Feeling**

Singer/Songwriters: Black Eye Peas

Scene 8

Song: **Free (Mood II Swing radio Edit)**

Songwriters: John Ciafone, Lem Soringsteen, Ultra Naté

Artist: Ultra Naté

Scene 9

Song: **Welcome Home**

Songwriter: Jean Alphonse Dupre

Artists: Peters and Lee

Song: **I Will Rise**

Songwriters: Lucinda Drayton and Marcus Cliffe

Artist: Lucinda Drayton

Lyric: *Where do I begin...*

Song: **Where Do I Begin**

Songwriters: Carl Sigman and Francis Lai

Artist: Andy Williams

Lyric: *Sisters are doing it for themselves*

Song: **Sisters Are Doing It For Themselves**

Songwriters: Annie Lennox, Dave Stewart

Artists: Aretha Franklin, Annie Lennox

Finale

Song: **Get Happy**
Songwriters: Harold Arlen and Ted Koehler
Artist: Judy Garland

Foyer Chit-Chat

Lyric: *The way that she moves to her own beat*
Song: **She's Royal**
Songwriter: Omar Riley
Artist: Tarrus Riley

Outro

Lyric: *Sealed with a kiss*
Song: **Sealed With A Kiss**
Songwriters: Gary Geld and Peter Udell
Artist: Brian Hyland

BONUS:

The ROYL Dance Playlist!

To receive the free playlist that had Pearl dance crazy 'jump and wave' during her writing, sign up here: www.pearljordan/author

BOOK REFERENCES

A Return to Love, Reflections On The Principles Of A Course In Miracles by Marianne Williamson

You Can Heal Your Life by Louise L Hay

Messages From The Body by Narayan-Singh, edited by Lynne R Henderson

Of Water And The Spirit — Ritual, Magic, And Initiation In The Life of An African Shaman by Malidoma Patrice Somé

Moon Time – The Art Of Harmony With Nature And Lunar Cycles by Johanna Paungger and Thomas Poppe

Women Who Run With The Wolves — Contacting The Power of The Wild Woman by Clarissa Pinkola Estés

Feel The Fear And Do It Anyway by Susan Jeffers

Healing the Wounds of Slave Trade and Slavery Approaches & Practices: UNESCO, A Desk Review, June 2020

The Anthology of American Jazz Dance by Gus Giordano

The Untethered Soul by Michael A. Singer

The Artist's Way — A Course in Discovering and Recovering Your Creative Self by Julia Cameron

Collage As A Creative Coaching Tool – A Comprehensive Resource for Coaches and Psychologists by Andréa Watts

ABOUT THE AUTHOR

Pearl Jordan is a former jazz dancer and choreographer whose life was ticking along nicely when she felt the 'niggles' — soul nudges highlighting that it was time for change, time for a new dance, on the stage of life. She found that other women were also looking to find a 'new beat' to reconnect to their authentic rhythm, and to the heart of who they are.

So inspired was Pearl by these transformational conversations, she felt the call to write a book. This would mean overcoming one of her deeply rooted fears: writing! To her astonishment, she scribed lyrically, creatively and powerfully, bringing high points of awareness, insight and change.

Pearl is founder of the innovative Rhythmic Remedy® — where personal and professional growth meets dance. Through coaching, workshops and professional speaking, Pearl guides women who are in transition, feeling confused about who they are and what they want, to lightly dance into the next phase of their life feeling confident, energised and fully connected to the rhythm of their soul.

Follow Pearl on:

Instagram @theroyalpearljordan

LinkedIn pearljordan.com

Website pearljordan.com

YOUR INSPIRATIONS

www.ingramcontent.com/pod-product-compliance
Lightning Source LLC
Chambersburg PA
CBHW061229070526
44584CB00030B/4041